C000205742

The Wc

The Wondrous Cross

Atonement and Penal Substituion in the Bible and History

Stephen R. Holmes

LONDON ● COLORADO SPRINGS ● HYDERABAD

Copyright © 2007 Stephen R. Holmes

13 12 11 10 09 08 07   7 6 5 4 3 2 1

First published in 2007 by Paternoster
Paternoster is an imprint of Authentic Media
9 Holdom Avenue, Bletchley, Milton Keynes, Bucks, MK1 1QR
1820 Jet Stream Drive , Colorado Springs, CO 80921, USA
OM Authentic Media, Medchal Road, Jeedimetla Village,
Secunderabad 500 055, A.P., India
www.authenticmedia.co.uk
Authentic Media is a division of IBS-STL UK, a company limited by guarantee
(registered charity no. 270162)

British Library Cataloguing in Publication Data

A catalogue record for this book is available from
the British Library.

ISBN-13 978-1-84227-541-2
ISBN-10 1-84227-541-0

Extract from 'Come and See' by Graham Kendrick © 1989 Make Way Music.
www.grahamkendrick.co.uk. Used by permission.
Extract from 'We Sing Your Mercies' by Mark Alrogge © 1997 Sovereign Grace
Praise administered by Copy Care, PO Box 77, Hailsham, BN27 3EF, UK.
Enquiries@copycare.com. Used by permission.
Extracts from 'Who Can Ever Say' by Dave Bilbrough; 'For the Cross' by Matt
and Beth Redman; and 'With a Prayer' by Stuart Townend © 1989, 1998, 2002
Thankyou Music administered by worshiptogether.com songs, exclusive UK
and Europe, administered by kingswaysongs.com. tym@kingsway.co.uk. Used
by permission.
Cover design by fourninezero design.
Print Management by Adare Carwin
Printed in Great Britain by J.H. Haynes and Co., Sparkford

Contents

for Judith and Philippa

'Crucifixion to the World through the Cross of Christ'

When I survey the wondrous cross
Where the young Prince of Glory died,
My richest gain I count but loss,
And pour contempt on all my pride.

Forbid it, Lord, that I should boast,
Save in the death of Christ my God:
All the vain things that charm me most,
I sacrifice them to his blood.

See from his head, his hands, his feet,
Sorrow and love flow mingled down!
Did e'er such love and sorrow meet,
Or thorns compose so rich a crown?

His dying crimson, like a robe,
Spreads o'er his body on the tree;
Then am I dead to all the globe
And all the globe is dead to me.

Were the whole realm of nature mine,
That were a present far too small;
Love so amazing, so divine,
Demands my soul, my life, my all.

(Isaac Watts, 1707)

This hymn was sung at my baptism in St Andrews Street Baptist Church, Cambridge, in 1992. In the second edition of his hymn-book (1709), Watts changed the second line to 'On which the prince . . .', which undoubtedly improved the scansion, and marked the fourth verse as optional, which undoubtedly weakened the theology. The title is Watts's.

Preface

Like so much else does, this book began with friends. Colin Gunton, Ann Holt, and David Coffey each told me I should be writing something on penal substitution; Ian Randall, Joel Edwards, and David Hilborn in different ways encouraged me to believe that my initial academic efforts might be worth translating into a more accessible format. None of them, of course, is responsible for what I have said. And I am fairly sure that at one point or another – even in some cases on the main point of the book – each would disagree strongly. Alan Torrance and John Colwell will not like some of what I have written, I suspect, but have made it much better than it might have been by their probing and gracious questioning at various points. Robin Parry of Paternoster has been, as always, encouraging and helpful, and was astonishingly generous with deadlines when I discovered I had greatly over-committed myself with a new home, a new job, and several pressing demands. Nicky Grieshaber's editorial work improved the book at every turn.

One of the themes of this book is that it is the task of theologians (and preachers) to try to articulate what the Christian community already knows. I cannot imagine doing what I do were it not for the local churches who have welcomed our family and sustained us with their worship, life and witness. To Ashford Baptist Church and my erstwhile fellow leaders there, Ian Morris, Anne Balfour, Simon Shutt and John Belstead, and to St Andrews Baptist Church and our pastor Liam Garvie, I offer heartfelt and public, if inadequate, thanks.

The book is dedicated to our daughters, Judith and Philippa, who have become rather too used to seeing Daddy behind a laptop, or to not seeing him at all because he's in a different room working. I regularly find myself praying that my deficiencies as a father might be made up by the fact that they have such a wonderful mother, and my gratitude to, and love for, Heather only increases with the passing of time.

A couple of notes about the text. Because the book is intended for a general audience, I have not put in references very often. All should be fairly easy to track down for anyone interested. All Bible quotations are my own translations, no doubt owing something to the memory of the NRSV and the NIV, which are the versions I habitually use.

S.R.H.
St Mary's College, St Andrews
All Saints Day, 2006

One

'Beneath the Cross of Jesus'

Beneath the Cross of Jesus I fain would take my stand . . .
Oh safe and happy shelter! Oh refuge tried and sweet!
Oh trysting place, where heaven's love and heaven's justice meet!
(Elizabeth Clephane, 'Beneath the Cross of Jesus')

Standing Under the Cross

Christians have always been more concerned to stand under the cross than to understand it. And rightly so. The cross is right at the heart of Christian faith and life. In one of the earliest of the New Testament books, Paul demands an astonishingly single-minded focus on the cross: 'Jews demand miraculous signs while Greeks look for wisdom – but we preach Christ crucified' (1 Cor. 1:22); 'Whilst I was among you, I resolved to know nothing but Jesus Christ and him crucified' (1 Cor. 2:1–2); 'Christ crucified is the wisdom of God and the power of God' (1 Cor. 1:23–24). Christ crucified – the message of the cross – is central to Christian life and thought and must remain so. Without the cross, there is no Christianity, and there can certainly be no Christians. Without the cross, there would be no possibility of a company of forgiven, redeemed people joyfully celebrating their salvation. Without the cross, our experience of life would be nothing but sin and shame.

The *worship* of Christian churches is – or should be – cross-centred. 'Do you not know,' asks Paul, 'that all those of us who were baptised into Christ Jesus were baptised into his death?' (Rom. 6:3). We begin our Christian lives confessing our hope and trust in the death of Christ, and praying for the gift of God's Spirit to enable us to live constantly in the light of that. As we continue to come to worship, at the heart of what we do is a commemoration of the death of Christ, sharing symbols of his broken body and poured out blood, praying that by God's Spirit the benefits of his death will be made real in our lives. What do we have to sing about, except the love of God made real in the cross of Jesus? How can we dare to come to the Father in prayer for the world and expect to be heard unless we can plead Jesus' death?

The preaching of Christian churches is – or should be – cross-centred. 'Jews demand miraculous signs and Greeks look for wisdom – but we preach Christ crucified' (1 Cor. 1:22–23). The great Swiss theologian Karl Barth tells the story of when he was still committed to a liberal theology that had forgotten the cross, how he looked out of his study window and realised that he had nothing to say to the people, that he knew no reason why they should come to hear him preach.

And there was no reason. Without the cross the church – and every preacher in the church – really does have nothing to say. Absolutely nothing. Platitudes about the goodness of God are empty and worthless unless we can point to the cross of Jesus as proof of God's great victory over evil, God's refusal to let all the suffering and sin in the world be the final word. Moral teaching is not just meaningless but positively cruel, nothing more than a loading of crushing burdens on already broken backs, unless we can point sinful people to a power outside themselves which can enable them to be the people they long to be – and there is no power that can do this, nothing in all creation, except the cross of Christ.

The life of Christian disciples is – or should be – cross-centred. 'Deny yourself, take up your cross, and follow me!' commanded the Lord (Mk 8:34); 'Your attitude should be the same as that of Christ Jesus who . . . humbled himself . . . and became obedient unto death – even death on a cross,' advised the apostle Paul (Phil. 2:5–8).

Our constant longing to be different people brings us always to the cross, to the place where we can confess our failure and shame and sin and know the glorious freedom of being released from it all by the gift of God. John's Gospel tells us we have the power of the Spirit in our lives only because Jesus went to the cross: 'The Spirit was not yet given, because Jesus was not glorified' (Jn 7:39) – and Jesus' glorification always refers to the cross in John. And Peter's very first sermon, in which he explained the gift of the Spirit on the first Pentecost, took his hearers straight back to the cross of Jesus (Acts 2:23).

Despite all this, there has been an amazing diversity in the ways that Christians have tried to understand what Jesus did for us on the cross. From the first, Christians have known and celebrated the glorious liberation, the new life and hope, that flow from Calvary. We have not needed to *understand* how Jesus' death gives us all the riches of the new birth and life that God by his Spirit offers in Christ, so long as we have known the reality of it.

Still today we see in the life of new converts the power of Jesus made real even though they have little understanding of why it comes to them. I remember in my own life the overwhelming sense of freedom and joy flooding through me the night I first made a step of commitment at a University Christian Union mission, despite the fact that I understood nothing then of what Jesus had done. This is what I mean when I say that Christians have always been more concerned to stand under the cross than to understand it. It matters that our lives are touched, transformed, by it, not that we can explain how it can transform.

Trying to Understand

All that said, however, there is a place for trying to understand. When we celebrate the cross in prayer and song, when we proclaim the cross in preaching, we need to find words that are, if not adequate (what words could ever be adequate? All eternity will not be long enough to praise Jesus the Saviour for what he has done!), at least honouring. Those of us who preach need to study and think so that when we call people to put their trust in the work of Jesus, we describe it well enough for them to be able to understand the gospel invitation. Songwriters need to work diligently to produce songs that are of such a nature that when we sing our praises to the risen Lord, we do so in ways that honour

him. Those who shape and lead public prayer need to teach their
people to speak rightly of God.

Just as we will never understand the mystery of the Trinity, or
how Christ can be both truly divine and truly human, so we will,
of course, never truly understand the indescribable gift of God in
Jesus and his cross. ('In vain the firstborn seraph tries to sound
the depths of love divine. 'Tis mystery all, let earth adore, let
angel minds enquire no more!') But just as we have learnt that
some ways of talking are inadequate to articulate these other
mysteries, serving only to dishonour God and obscure the wonders of what he has done, so the same might be true of ways of
talking about the cross.

This book is an attempt to examine one particular way of talking about the cross: that of referring to it in terms of penal substitution. I am looking at penal substitution because recently there
have been many arguments about it. Some faithful Christian
teachers have insisted that no discussion of the cross can be adequate unless it includes this way of talking; others, equally faithful, that any talk like this is dishonouring to God. Which is right,
and why? These are the questions I will try to answer.

The term *penal substitution* denotes a way of talking about the
cross in terms of crime and punishment: we have broken God's
law, and deserve to be punished for that, but God in his love provides a substitute, his own Son, who will take the punishment so
that we don't have to. As a result, we are freed from guilt and
enabled to become children of God. Chapters four and five will
discuss the history of Christian thinking about the cross in more
detail, but historians generally agree that the sixteenth-century
Reformer John Calvin was the first to give a full-blown penal
substitutionary account of the atonement. Since Calvin's day the
idea has become so important in Reformed and evangelical theology that it has often been seen as one of the touchstones of
orthodoxy. From Charles Hodge in nineteenth-century Princeton
to evangelical mission agencies today, the demand has been that
the cross must be thought about in penal substitutionary terms.
Doctrinal statements have demanded it, and Christian organisa-
tions have been split over it.

At the same time, others have objected to the idea of penal substitution as an idea:

- Liberal theologians in the nineteenth century objected to the idea that God could not simply forgive us out of love without any need for punishment. There is a telling example of this in L.W. Grensted's *A Short History of the Doctrine of the Atonement*, first published in 1920: Grensted repeatedly claims that penal accounts of the atonement are morally repugnant in their view of God, and rejoices openly that he can tell his history as if such theology was almost forgotten.

- In the twentieth century feminist theologians opened up a new line of criticism, suggesting that for God to punish his innocent Son amounted to nothing more than a legitimisation of child abuse. In their writings we find the notion that the cross of Jesus understood in broadly penal terms displays the sado-masochism of Christianity and as encourages abused women to become complicit in their abuse.

I will address both these lines of criticism in chapter eight, but for a long while they remained criticisms from people outside of the evangelical churches. Within the evangelical movement, we knew that this was what we believed about the cross, and defended it. Occasional voices might be raised in question or protest, but, broadly, the position held.

In the past few years, however, this has changed. Respected evangelical scholars and leaders have published books which do not merely express doubt about whether penal substitution is the best way of talking about the cross, but attack the tradition in the strongest possible terms. It is condemned as unbiblical, immoral, misleading, and damaging to Christian evangelism. The charge that it obscures the love of God, once pressed only by self-confessed liberals, is being heard from the most respected evangelical lips. Even the shocking suggestion that this is merely a cosmic act of child abuse has been borrowed from radical feminist critics and deployed within the camp.

Some welcome this trend as a much-needed purification; others see it as the surrendering of a vital aspect of Christian truth. Who is right? Or is there a mediating position which can recognise truth on both sides? These are the questions I intend to answer.

Telling Stories about the Cross

Before everything else, though, I want to flag up one idea that will be central to all the discussion that follows. It is what I call the 'stories of salvation' (or 'multiple models') way of talking about the cross. I will have much more to say about telling stories about the cross in the course of the book, but let me make clear what I mean right from the start.

Story is a slippery word: at its worst, it suggests something childish and probably untrue. I hope it is obvious that this is not the sense in which I use the word. Jesus told many, many parables, and used them to point to truths so deep and profound that they could not be put into words other than the words of a story. Stories are ways of making sense of the world, and of God. They are ways of illuminating how God deals with his children which capture the richness of personal interaction. Logical arguments are very important, but we will not get hold of what it means to talk about God's love, or mercy (or anger or wrath for that matter) by logic alone: we need to tell stories. If it helps someone to think *parable* whenever I write *story*, then I don't have a problem with that . . .

As I have said, and shall explore in more detail in chapter six, there has been a marked shift in the way theologians have talked about the cross in recent decades. A century ago, almost all theologians were agreed that there was one best way of describing the cross, although they disagreed on what it might be. Evangelicals would insist on penal substitution, and Liberals on moral influence, but both were sure that only one could be right. A ground-breaking book by the Swedish theologian Gustav Aulén, *Christus Victor* (1930), argued that the first Christians had thought of the cross neither in moral nor in penal categories, but in terms of Christ's victory over the evil powers. Aulén was still sure, however, that there was only one right way of talking about the cross; he just had a new view of what that way was. In more recent years most theologians writing on the atonement have rejected this notion that there is only one right way; instead they suggest that there are many different pictures or models which each illuminate something of the event of Calvary, but which need one another – none is sufficient on its own.

In view of this the question is not whether talk of penal substitution is better than talk of victory, but how adequate each picture is. We might find that both are helpful ways of discussing the cross, or neither is.

This seems to me to be a vital insight, for several reasons.

To start with, the New Testament does not confine itself to one set of images or ideas when it discusses the cross. Instead, even individual verses pile different images on top of one another in a sometimes bewildering mix.

I will say more about this in chapter three, but for now consider a classic text like Romans 3:24–25: 'All . . . are justified freely by his grace through the redemption that came by Christ Jesus. God presented him as an atoning sacrifice . . .' Paul uses three different pictures of the atonement just in these few words: *justified* is a legal term, talking about the doing away of guilt; *redemption* is a term borrowed from the slave-market, and speaks of the setting free of someone sold into a lifetime of bondage; and *sacrifice* is a term that recalls the entire Old Testament tradition of the offering of blood on the altar. This mixing of metaphors is common within the New Testament and so, I suggest, should be normal within our theology.

The first theologians in the early church (which we will look at in chapter four), presumably following the biblical witness, offered similarly rich combinations of different themes, and the same is true of the great theologians of the later tradition. John Calvin, for instance, who gave us the first full statement of penal substitution, combines it with ideas of victory, sacrifice, intercession, and several others. (There is more on Calvin in chapter five.)

It is not just biblical and historical examples that prove the point, however. As I shall explore in chapter six, there seem to be good theological reasons for thinking of the cross in terms of many metaphors. The event of Calvary is unique. It is not just one in a series of similar acts of inspirational self-sacrifice, nor is it an example of a more general principle of law in operation. Rather, the cross is so fundamental to any properly Christian account of relationship, justice, love and a host of other human experiences that it cannot be described exhaustively in these ways. We just do not know what self-sacrifice means until we see Jesus on the cross. The same is true of justice. If we think we know what self-sacrifice is, or what justice is, or whatever, and then force the cross to fit our understanding, we end up getting things the wrong way up; instead, we need to realise that we will understand these things only when we understand them through the cross.

And so, if we are attempting to describe the cross and what Jesus was doing for us there, we need to grab hold of all these realities that are themselves defined by the cross, and tell stories about them.

But we cannot tell just one story and assume that that will do; if we try to do that, we will end up making the cross only an example of some more fundamental human experience, rather than the most fundamental thing in the whole of human history – or indeed any other part of history. Because Jesus does offer himself up in self-sacrifice on the cross, we need to talk about Jesus' death in sacrificial terms – partly because what we know about sacrifices will help us make sense of that death, but also because we will begin to understand what sacrifice, and self-sacrifice, really mean only when we see them fulfilled and transformed in Jesus.

What I will be arguing in this book is that this 'many metaphors' picture of how to talk about the cross is the only way to understand penal substitution. If we start thinking that this is a complete and exhaustive account of exactly what was going on at the cross, then we will miss much of what Scripture has to say about the glories of Jesus' death, and we will need to force some of the rest out of shape in order to make it fit the scheme that we are imposing. It doesn't matter how clever we are; our minds are not capable of creating boxes big enough that we can fit God within them. I do think, however, that if we are prepared to accept that penal substitution is one very powerful metaphor, one story that will help us to illuminate aspects of the wonderful thing that Jesus has done for us, then we can and should continue to hold on to it.

Understood like this, penal substitution is a metaphor, a story, that will make things clearer and help us better confess the joy of salvation. As we start to use language borrowed from the law court to talk about Jesus' death, it will also challenge our understandings of law and justice. When we look at this death in terms

of law and justice, we will be challenged to rethink all our ideas
of justice and law, to align them more closely with the revelation
of the truth about the world in Jesus Christ.

How to Argue, or 'Getting Cross about the Cross' – the place of Love

As I have said, I will make this argument in much more detail
throughout the rest of the book, looking at biblical, theological
and historical reasons for holding to it, and so on. I am, however,
conscious that even as I write, an argument is simmering
throughout British evangelicalism at least about the appropriate-
ness of speaking of the cross of Jesus in penal substitutionary
terms. I had intended to write about penal substitution before I
ever became aware of this argument, and indeed I published an
academic paper on the subject at about the time I was first becoming conscious that something was going on amongst people
whom I admired, or regarded as friends (on both sides of the
debate).

For me it all began at an academic conference where it seemed
as though everyone who spoke began by noting with gratitude
that the barbaric old idea of penal substitution was now dead and
buried. At the time I had no strong views about penal substitution: the people who had taught me theology seemed not to think
it very useful or important, and so I hadn't given it a lot of
thought.

However, as over four days of conference I listened to it being
repeatedly rubbished, it occurred to me that some, at least, of the
songs my church sang needed a lot of editing if these people were
right. So at the end of the conference, in an open discussion, I
made a few comments, trying to defend the idea in the face of the
derision I had encountered. I later discovered that one of the
speakers at that conference was perhaps the most outspoken
critic of penal substitution in the world today; it was probably
good that I didn't know that at the time . . . I guess this history
has coloured the way I approach the subject. I did not come to the
question with a strong awareness of an evangelical orthodoxy
that needed dethroning or defending. Instead, I came to it in the

context of a wider theological scene that assumed the doctrine had been destroyed long ago, and so never bothered to understand what it claimed, or why it might be wrong. However, the shape of this book was conceived with the current debate amongst evangelicals – my friends – in mind. I want to make a contribution to that debate, but I do not want to win it. To 'win' implies there will be losers, a drive for conquest that is wholly out of keeping with discussions about the cross of Christ. The cross brings reconciliation, and good theology about the cross should similarly be reconciling. I will not address the most recent debate directly in the body of the book (although I discuss some of the most important books at the end); but I do attempt to take seriously the needs of both sides.

Most importantly, it is vital that we do not become like Cromwell's followers as they are described in the classic humorous telling of English history *1066 and All That* . . . There, W.C Sellar and R.J. Yeatman describe the Roundheads as 'right but repulsive'! This has been a constant danger for us as evangelicals. We know that we hold to the truth about Jesus, and so we can sometimes become smug or aggressive or unpleasant towards those who do not understand the truth. But the truth about the saviour Jesus is never unpleasant or repulsive; it is beautiful, winsome, attractive, alluring, and arresting. And so must our theology – and particularly our preaching – be beautiful and winsome and alluring and the rest. We are called to live in cheerful, self-deprecating hopefulness. Zealous for truth, yes, but always remembering that God can look after his own interests and doesn't really need our help, and so refusing to take ourselves too seriously. This is the proper attitude for a Christian thinker or preacher or believer. Most vitally, we are called to love one another – it is love between Christians that will convince the world that the gospel is true, according to John 17:23.

Love does not mean we never disagree, of course – just think about your family! Heather and I had the privilege of being prepared for marriage by a wise and gracious Christian couple who once said to us that when engaged couples came saying, 'Oh, we've never had an argument . . .' they wanted to say, 'Well, go and have one, and then come back and we'll continue the marriage preparation . . .' As Christians we will disagree. But love should mark the way we disagree. Paul talks about it in Romans 14, where love for brothers and sisters becomes far more important than being right about theological issues.

I had to learn this lesson in my own studies once. I am a Baptist pastor and theologian and I believe that the biblical and proper way is to baptise believers who have confessed their faith, not newborn children. I remember once thinking that there must have been a moment when the early church switched from the practice of baptising only believing converts to infant baptism, and that it might be instructive to look at how they handled the questions that must have been around then. What I found astonished me – although it shouldn't have. Perhaps the greatest thinkers of Western and Eastern churches asked questions about the possibility of some people in the church ending up baptised twice and others ending up not baptised at all. And they gave exactly the same answer: the bond of love matters more than questions about the validity of baptisms. I looked at Augustine in the (Latin-speaking) Western church and Basil the Great in the (Greek-speaking) Eastern church. They both had advice for dealing with baptismal questions, of course, but they were both prepared to accept that the pastoral pressures would result in some people in the church being twice-baptised and others being potentially not baptised at all. And they both said that the love and unity of the church mattered more than any of that. Truth matters – these great theologians knew that – truth matters, but truth without love is so far from anything Christian that it has ceased to be truth. Christian theologians can never be 'right but repulsive': if they are repulsive, they are so far from Jesus and his gospel as to be just plain wrong.

'If I speak in human and angelic tongues, if I speak prophecies and can fathom all mysteries, if my witness to truth is so strong that I end up martyred, but I have not love, I am nothing – I have nothing. Only a noisy gong, or a clanging cymbal.' So says Paul in 1 Corinthians 13. (Anthony Thiselton, in one of the best commentaries on 1 Corinthians, gives several pages of very learned discussion as to what instruments the Greek words translated gong and cymbal might be, before concluding that the best way to translate the passage might be with an old Yorkshire saying: 'if I have not love, I am nowt but wind and rattle'!)

This need to have and show love must be true for theology and preaching as well. However profound our grasp of the Bible, however powerful our logical arguments, however comprehensive our knowledge of Christian history and thought, however funny and moving our illustrations, if we do not love, then all we say, all we write, is still 'nowt but wind and rattle'. Theology cannot be done apart from discipleship, and the core of discipleship is love: 'God is love, and whoever lives in love lives in God, and God in them' (1 Jn. 4:16). More than that: 'Whoever does not love does not know God, for God is love' (1 Jn. 4:8).

This Book

The rest of this book will look like this:

Chapters two and three will look at the biblical pictures of the cross: Old Testament pictures in chapter two and New Testament in chapter three. In chapter two I will talk about how the Old Testament can be used to find pictures of the cross. Then I will focus particularly on the different accounts of sacrifice we find in the Old Testament: the commands in the Law that sacrifice should be offered; the presence of sacrifice even outside the Law; and the criticisms of trusting too much in sacrifices that we find in the prophets and Psalms. After that I will look at other possible Old Testament pictures of the cross, particularly in Isaiah 53. In chapter three I will show that the New Testament writers use all sorts of different pictures when talking about the cross, and I will use this to suggest that my idea about using 'many metaphors' remains important. The central New Testament metaphors are sacrifice, victory and ransom, but there are others too (including penal substitution).

After the biblical material I will turn to examine teaching about the cross in Christian history. Chapter four will look at the first 1,500 years – all the time before the Reformation. For almost the first 1,000 years of the church there wasn't much sustained reflection on the mechanics of the cross; what there was often came in passing, using the undisputed fact of redemption through the cross of Jesus to prove some other point (perhaps about the true humanity of Jesus). Notions of ransom and victory were fairly common, as was an idea that Jesus had transformed the 'stuff' human beings are made out of by taking it to the cross and through death to resurrection.

In the Middle Ages, Anselm of Canterbury introduced the idea of 'satisfaction': that somehow Christ's death fills up a lack that was caused by our sins. Anselm was opposed by Peter Abelard, who rather saw the cross as an inspirational act of self-sacrifice.

In chapter five I turn to the Reformation and after. Generally, John Calvin is credited with providing the first complete statement of a penal substitutionary theory of the atonement, although a generation earlier Martin Luther had begun to move in that direction. This doctrine was opposed, however, by other strands of the Reformation, notably the Anabaptists, and of course by the Roman Catholic counter-reformation.

After the Reformation these positions were strengthened and more carefully spelled out for a while in the period known as 'Reformed Orthodoxy'. At the same time, the cross was preached powerfully to the unconverted during the Evangelical Revival, with penal substitutionary ideas to the fore.

In the nineteenth century, however, things changed. Under the influence of the great Friedrich Schleiermacher, a new 'liberal' theology emerged, which rejected penal substitution and replaced it with the idea that the death of Jesus was simply an inspiring act of self-sacrifice. Charles Hodge and other Princeton theologians rejected this very strongly, however, as did more traditional theologians in Europe.

In the twentieth century the movement known as 'neo-ortho-doxy' offered complex and sometimes compelling reconstructions of classical Christian ideas about the atonement. Some of these people were hospitable to penal substitution, others less so.

At the same time, a new interest in the history of doctrine led to attempts to revive all but forgotten patristic ideas (most famously in Gustav Aulén's *Christus Victor*, which I've already mentioned).

In the latter half of the twentieth century, liberationist or feminist theologies offered both new visions of the atonement of Jesus and powerful critiques of some of the traditional Christian ways of talking about it, not least penal substitution.

After all this history, in chapter six I develop my own thinking of how we should talk rightly about the cross. I discuss different ways of thinking about theories of the cross as 'metaphors', and whether we should be looking for the one right version, or for a way, rather, of holding several accounts together. Here I offer my most sustained defence of what I have called the 'many metaphors' idea.

In chapter seven I turn to trying to develop a statement of penal substitution that takes seriously the various criticisms that have been put forward against this theory. I do believe that a careful statement can answer most of them, and here I try to show how.

In chapter eight I look particularly at some criticisms of penal substitution that have been common recently, and try to show how they can be answered if the idea is properly understood.

In chapter nine I look at the use of penal substitutionary metaphors for the atonement, showing how they teach us ethical principles, help us in our work of evangelism and making the good news of Jesus known, and inspire us to discipleship, to a properly holy Christian life.

Finally, I look at a couple of famous attacks on penal substitution from current evangelical scholars or leaders and try to assess the strengths and weaknesses of the various arguments they offer.

We begin, however, where Christian theology, if it is to be adequately Christian, must always begin and end: with the inspired Scriptures, the Word of God.

Two

'Promised in the Faithful Word'

The Cross in the Old Testament

This is He whom Saints in old time
Chanted of with one accord;
Whom the voices of the prophets
Promised in the faithful word.
            (Aurelius Prudentius, 'Of the Father's Love Forgotten')

The Cross in the Old Testament

There is, of course, a problem in talking about the cross in the Old Testament. The New Testament writers were trying to explain something that had happened, a historical event they could remember, point to, and discuss. They knew about the cross. The Old Testament writers didn't – or at least not in the same way.

The Bible itself tells us about this problem – more than once. Peter, in his first letter, comments that the prophets struggled to see what, by the Spirit, they were prophesying about (1 Pet. 1:10–12); Jesus himself tells his disciples that 'prophets and righteous people longed to see' what they were seeing – Jesus, present amongst them – but didn't (Mt. 13:17).

Now, when it comes to the prophets, of course, it is easy, or at least fairly easy. They spoke of things that were to come, at least some of the time, and the life and death and resurrection and coming reign of Jesus are the fulfilment of their prophecies, or so the New Testament claims (Lk. 18:31 or 24:25–27; Jn 1:45).

Sometimes it can be quite hard to work out how the prophecies should be interpreted or applied, of course. I was at a local retreat

centre recently, and the warden was telling me she had been at a
service where the preacher had read a prophecy from Isaiah 18
about people travelling in 'paper boats', and then didn't explain
it at all during his sermon. She missed most of what he did say,
because she was trying to work out what this was about. Even
when we struggle with a particular passage like this, though, we
know how prophecy should work!

Types

But there is a lot in the Old Testament that isn't prophecy, and
some of it, at least, is taken up by the New Testament to speak of
the cross and resurrection. Jesus himself at one point talks about
the 'sign of Jonah', seemingly suggesting that just as Jonah spent
three days in the belly of a fish, and then emerged, so he would
go into the tomb and come out on the third day. The book of
Jonah doesn't record this strange event as a prophecy, not even an
acted out prophecy like some of Ezekiel's (e.g. Ezek. 4). Instead,
it is an event in the life of a prophet, a part of his story, that suddenly becomes an illustration or something of what would happen to Jesus. Should we take the whole of Jonah's story to be
some sort of prophecy of the life of Christ? And if Jonah's, who
else's? Job's? Abraham's? David's?

The practice of finding stories in the Old Testament that somehow prefigure the salvation won by Jesus is a common one in
Christian history. Some of our best hymns do it. 'Guide me O
thou great Jehovah', for example, uses the desert wanderings
that followed the exodus from Egypt as an image of Christian
life, with the final entry into the promised land by crossing the
Jordan being an image of the Christian passing through death
into heaven:

> When I tread the verge of Jordan,
> bid my anxious fears subside.
> Death of death, and hell's destruction,
> land me safe on Canaan's side.

The same image is there in the great Easter hymn 'Thine be the
Glory', which ends: 'Bring us safe through Jordan, to thy home
above.'

This is called 'typology': a 'type' is an event in the Old Testament that prefigures something about the life of Jesus, like Jonah's three days in the fish.

There are two problems with interpreting the Bible like this.

The first problem is that although preachers and spiritual writers have never stopped doing it, it became quite suspect in good academic circles. It wasn't the proper way to read the Bible, apparently. This is now changing a bit, thankfully, and there has been quite a lot of interest in recovering methods like this of reading the Old Testament as a Christian text. For various reasons, the academics are getting back to what the preachers always knew: that if the Bible is to be interesting in church it must be heard – there at least – as a specifically Christian writing. So people are becoming interested again in ways of reading the Old Testament that find Christ in all the Scriptures.

The second problem is perhaps more difficult: there are a few examples of 'types' in the New Testament, like the Jonah text, but how do we decide what else works as a type? Is it just the things that the New Testament tells us, or can we read other texts like this? Some passages, after all, seem to invite this reading; they just look like fairly obvious candidates for hearing in a Christian way.

One example might be all the sacrifices, but even here it becomes a little complicated – after all, God has quite a lot to say through the prophets and psalms about the problems of people relying on sacrifices, and how they are not that important. Should we apply all that to the death of Jesus as well?

The Old Testament sacrifices

Sacrifice is a big theme in the Old Testament, but not a wholly positive one. It is also a common theme in other religious traditions. It seems that, instinctively, most human people have felt the need to make offerings to whatever god they have believed in. Anthropologists, who study the varieties of human culture, have noticed just how common sacrifice is, in one form or another. We shouldn't assume, though, that the sacrifices in the Old Testament are just like any other human sacrifices. They might be similar, but God commands most of them, and we need to listen to what God says about what they mean in order to understand properly what is going on.

Did God command sacrifices?

God commands most of the sacrifices in the Old Testament, but there are some that, apparently, he didn't. Most of the sacrifices in Genesis, coming as they do before God gives the law (and with it the rules for sacrifice), appear to be instinctive human responses as much as obedience to divine commands. When we look at the first sacrifices in the Bible, those of Cain and Abel, there is no suggestion that God ordered them to sacrifice in a particular way. They did it because it seems to be something natural for human beings to do. And somehow, mysteriously, Abel sacrificed well, but Cain sacrificed badly (Gen. 4:4–5).

This is a theme that runs through the Old Testament: that some sacrifices are acceptable to God, while others are an affront to him. That early in Genesis there is no hint why that should be so, but it is already an important recognition: sacrifice does not work like a slot machine on a station platform, where you put the right stuff in the slot at the beginning and get the blessing you wanted out at the end. Sacrifice is, in some complex way, about a relationship with God, a gift that the believer gives to God, perhaps, as a way of acknowledging and maintaining that relationship.

Noah offered a sacrifice to God after coming off the ark (Gen. 8:20). Abraham sacrificed to God more than once. In Genesis 15, God commands the sacrifice, and the sacrifice is somehow instrumental in God's making his covenant with Abraham.

In Genesis 22 we have the strange and powerful story of God demanding that Abraham sacrifice his only son, Isaac. This is clearly God's command (Gen. 22:2), yet in Genesis 22:11–12 God stops Abraham from making the sacrifice. Abraham then looks and sees a ram, and sacrifices that instead. Earlier, Isaac had asked where the animal for the sacrifice was (Gen. 22:7), and Abraham had answered that God would provide a 'lamb for the burnt offering'. The text does not quite state that the ram with its horns caught is God's provision, but we are probably supposed to read it like that – God gives a 'lamb' (Abraham's word) to be sacrificed so that Abraham's son may be spared.

It is difficult not to read this story as a type, or foreshadowing, of the death of Christ, surely? If we do, however, what does it mean? Isaac's life is not demanded because he had sinned, or because Abraham had sinned, or for any reason at all in the text. God will do what he would not make Abraham do, but the reason why it must be done by anyone remains hidden.

Notice also the assumption in Genesis 22 that sacrifice is normal. As they journey towards Moriah, Isaac looks around and recognises the standard paraphernalia of sacrifice, except the animal to be killed, and this is what he asks his father about. Although we do not read in Scripture of Abraham sacrificing often, clearly it is something normal enough for Isaac to recognise what is going on, whether because of his father's and family's practice, or because it is common in the culture around them. Like for other ancient peoples, sacrifice was a normal feature of Isaac's life, something he recognised when he saw it, just as we might see someone with a pack of beer and some sausages and a bag of charcoal and think, 'Barbeque tonight!'

Abraham's grandson, Jacob, offers a sacrifice after he and his father-in-law, Laban, have argued and then made up (Gen. 31:54). Here, the sacrifice is a ritual killing of an animal before it is eaten, a form of sacrifice that is common in the law later on. In the context of the narrative, however, it is more than that. Jacob has worked for Laban for twenty years, and married his two daughters, Leah and Rachel. Now, finally, he is leaving to go home, at God's command (Gen. 31:3) but it seems that he cannot bring himself to tell Laban that he is going – perhaps fearing the old man will find yet another excuse to keep him there. More than that, when Jacob tells his family to get ready to leave, Rachel steals the 'household gods', Laban's idols. Laban is understandably upset, and chases after Jacob, and there is something of an argument when they meet, with Laban accusing Jacob of ingratitude and theft, and Jacob pouring out the accumulated injustices of twenty years. Two symbolic acts seal the peace: the construction of a heap of stones, which seems in part to mark a boundary between the two families' land (Gen. 31:52), and the sacrifice, which is at least a mark of reconciliation between them, and perhaps something more.

In Exodus 18:12, Jethro, Moses' father-in-law, brings a sacrifice as a mark of thanksgiving for all that God has done in bringing the people of Israel out of Egypt. This is the last acceptable sacrifice in

Israel that is not directly commanded by God; the law is then given, and sacrifices have to conform to the commands God has given.

There is, however, one other place where we read of sacrifices not according to the law: Job 1:5, which tells us that Job sacrificed regularly. It seems that for Job the sacrifices were a preventative measure, designed to deal with the possibility that his children may have sinned against God. At the end of the book God commands Job's friends to ask Job to make sacrifice so that they may not suffer for their 'folly' (Job 42:8).

What do the sacrifices mean?

In the law that God gives to his people, many sacrifices are commanded, of course. For the day-to-day sacrifices, Leviticus 1–7 offers a complete code of how sacrifices are to be made, but there is not much here about the meaning of the sacrifices.

Some of them – but only some – are connected with forgiveness of sin (Lev. 4–6). After describing the regulations for the sacrifice the text says, repeatedly, something like 'the priest shall make atonement for them, and they shall be forgiven' (Lev. 4:20, 26, 31, 35; 5:6, 10, 13, etc.).

There is also the 'peace-offering' or 'sacrifice of well-being' (Lev. 3), which is not so much about dealing with sin as about giving thanks for God's goodness (Lev. 7:11–12), paying a vow (Lev. 22:21), or in some other way maintaining the worshipper's relationship with God.

Finally there is the 'burnt offering' (Lev. 1), which seems to function in all sorts of ways in the Old Testament. Sometimes it is about dealing with uncleanness or sin (Lev. 14:20); sometimes about seeking God's blessing. King Saul offers a burnt offering as a way of praying for God's blessing (1 Sam. 13:12), and although Samuel criticises him for it, his fault seems to be that he did not wait for a priest and made the offering himself, rather than that he used it as a way of praying.

Why do these sacrifices work? Leviticus does not give a direct answer, but there are three important hints.

The first is that burning sacrifices makes a 'pleasing odour' before God (Lev. 1:9, 13, 17, etc.): God is pleased with sacrifice.

The second is the importance of blood, particularly in the sin-offerings (Lev. 4:5–7, etc.). The clue to what this means is in

Leviticus 17:11, where, in the middle of explaining why blood is not to be eaten, God says to Moses, 'the life of the flesh is in the blood, and I have given it to you for making atonement for your lives on the altar . . .' There is some basic connection between blood and life, which means that blood is particularly suited for 'making atonement' – repairing relations between God and his people that have been damaged by sin and uncleanness.

The third hint is the fact that sacrifice becomes 'an abomination' (Lev. 7:18) if the commandments are not properly followed (as when King Saul makes his own sacrifice).

There is nothing automatic about sacrifice – God is not constrained to respond. It is not like clicking a computer icon. Instead, the sacrifices work because they are a part of the covenant God has established, a way he has graciously provided for relationships to be maintained and sin to be dealt with.

Feasts and sacrifices

Alongside these regular offerings are the great feasts of Israel, which all involve sacrifice (Lev. 23; Num. 28–29). Perhaps the two most important feasts for thinking about the work of Christ are the Passover and the Day of Atonement.

As we will see, all the gospels, in different ways, link the death of Jesus with the Passover celebration. The Passover begins in Egypt, when God sends the final terrible plague on Pharaoh and his people, the death of every firstborn son. God tells Moses and Aaron that each family of Israel should sacrifice a lamb and eat it, but first they are to smear some of the blood around the doors of their houses so that the slaughter will 'pass over' them and afflict only the Egyptians.

The Day of Atonement rituals are described in Leviticus 16. The high priest of Israel washes and offers sacrifice to purify himself from all sin and uncleanness and to make atonement. Then he takes two goats and chooses randomly between them. One goat is sacrificed as a sin-offering 'for the sanctuary' (Lev. 16:16); the other (the 'scapegoat') has all the sins of Israel laid on it (Lev. 16:21) and is then sent into the wilderness. The ritual of the Day of Atonement is all about dealing with sin, in part through sacrifice, in part through a symbolic or ritual transfer of sins on to an animal that then carries them outside the camp.

Criticism of sacrifices

There is one final feature of the Old Testament witness to sacrifice we need to notice, and that is the critique.

Psalmists (Ps. 51:16–17) and prophets (e.g., Is. 1:11–13; Amos 5:21–27) unite in denying that God is pleased by sacrifice. If we read these passages carefully, however, it is not that God has changed his mind about sacrifice. Rather, the prophets object to an assumption that a mechanical performance of the sacrifices will please God, even if divorced from obedience to his commands and concern for justice and righteousness.

Sacrifice and the death of Christ

Sacrifice in the Old Testament has many meanings. It maintains the relationship between God and the worshipper; covers over sin, pollution and guilt; acts as a witness, and perhaps a cause, of reconciliation between Jacob and Laban; and turns aside the judgement and wrath of God in the Passover. At times, as with Isaac, it seems to have no meaning or context at all, except the command of God. Sacrifice works because God has said it will work: sacrifices in disobedience to God, and the assumption that God is somehow bound by sacrifices, are both roundly condemned.

The New Testament unquestionably uses the Old Testament sacrificial system as a way of explaining how Christ's death makes a difference to believer's lives, and to the wider world.

In the gospels we have the connection with the Passover: for example, John calls Jesus 'the lamb of God, who takes away the sin of the world', and I'll look at some other texts in the next chapter. The most sustained reflection on sacrifice, however, is surely in Hebrews, which uses sacrifice in general, and the Day of Atonement in particular, to understand and explain the work of Christ.

But there is a problem here: for people who saw sacrifices regularly, who celebrated the Passover, these were helpful images to explain what Jesus had done in dying on the cross. But for anyone who has not grown up seeing the Temple sacrifices that God commanded, the fact that the Old Testament doesn't really explain how sacrifice works means that comparing the death of

Jesus to a sacrifice doesn't help very much with understanding his work on the cross. We can say that the death of Jesus *does* the things these sacrifices did (maintains our relationship with God; covers over pollution and guilt; brings reconciliation between human enemies; protects us from the wrath and vengeance of God), but we cannot say *why* it is needed. Could God not do these things without the shedding of blood, whether the blood of animals or his own? It seems not – but seeing the cross in the light of all the Old Testament sacrifices doesn't explain *why* not.

Other Pictures of the Cross in the Old Testament

The most obvious place to look for a theology of the cross in the Old Testament is Isaiah 52–53, of course. This passage belongs to the last of four similar passages in Isaiah, often called the 'servant songs' (Is. 42:1–7; 49:1–6; 50:4–9; 52:13–53:12). These songs build up a picture of a 'servant of the Lord' called to bring justice (42:1) and salvation (42:6–7) to the nations (not just for Israel). The servant has been shaped and equipped by God for this task (49:2; 50:4–5), and will work quietly (42:3–4) to accomplish the task. As the songs go on, it becomes clear that the servant suffers: he is 'deeply despised, abhorred' (49:7), and beaten, insulted, and spat upon (50:6). He can be called 'a man of suffering' (or of 'sorrows') (53:3), who is oppressed and afflicted unjustly (53:7–8). Eventually, the servant is killed (53:8–9).

The songs don't tell us much about the precise nature of the servant's suffering. Instead, by using a whole series of different images, they build up a picture of general and universal suffering. The last song, however, begins to interpret the servant's pain: it is not seen as merely meaningless injustice, but is understood as a sacrifice for sin (53:10). The servant suffers on behalf of others (53:4–6), bringing wholeness and healing (53:5) and righteousness (53:11) to the 'many' he suffered for. Further, the death of the servant is not the end of his story (53:10–12); somehow, beyond death, God will exalt and establish his servant.

In the songs, the servant is identified explicitly with Israel (49:3). But the picture has to be more complicated than that, because part of the servant's mission is to save Israel (49:5–6), and the last song in particular pictures the servant as *one person*, not as a nation or group.

The New Testament repeatedly identifies Jesus as the servant (Mt. 8:17; 12:17–21; Jn 12:38; Lk. 22:37; Acts 8:35; 1 Pet. 2:21–25; and other references). The suffering and death of the servant must then refer to the cross of Jesus. So on the cross, Jesus 'was wounded for our sins and crushed for our wrongdoing' (Is. 53:5); had 'the iniquity of us all' laid on him (53:6); was 'struck down for the sin of (God's) people' (53:8) and 'counted amongst the sinners' (53:12).

Again we can ask: Does this text help us to understand how atonement works? If, somehow, the wounding and death of Jesus brought peace and righteousness to us, then how did it do so?

Isaiah uses the technical language of sacrifice ('sin-offering' in 53:10), but as we have seen, that doesn't get us very far. The servant's work is clearly substitutionary – 'the Lord has placed the sin of us all on him' (53:6) – and there is an aspect of exchange: his wounds lead to our healing; his punishment to our wholeness (53:5). Isaiah 53 comes as close as anything in the Bible to teaching penal substitutionary atonement. Still, there is not a fully worked out theory here. But the servant in this text is repeatedly said to die for the sins and wrongdoings of others, and to the extent that this is explained, it is with moral and legal language. Laws have been broken, and wounding and punishment are due, but the servant bears them so that others may be righteous.

Alongside Isaiah 52–53, the text that the New Testament, and early Christian writings, see as foretelling and interpreting the death of Jesus most often is Psalm 22.

Jesus himself cries out the first words of this psalm from the cross (Mt. 27:46; Mk 15:34), but the gospels reference it far more than just this. The gospels pick up many details of the suffering described in the psalm and apply it to Jesus: mocking and shaking heads (Ps. 22:7; Mt 27:39; Mk 15:29; Lk 23:35); the cry of the psalmist's enemies, 'Let God deliver him!' on the lips of the watching crowd in Matthew (Ps. 22:8; Mt 27:43); the psalmist's words, 'my mouth is dried up' (22:15), echoed by Jesus (Jn 19:28). Furthermore, 'they have pierced my hands and my feet' (Ps. 22:16) foretells, of course, the crucifixion in all four gospels, and John (19:24) quotes verse 18 of the psalm about Jesus' clothing being divided and lots being cast, a detail that is recorded without direct reference to the psalm in the other gospels as well.

Psalm 22 is not the only psalm referenced by the gospel narratives. Psalm 69 is recalled in various ways, most obviously in 'they gave me vinegar to drink' (Ps. 69:21); and commentators find echoes of Psalms 27, 35, 37, 38, 39, 41, 54, 55 and 86 in Mark 14–15 alone! The Psalms, of course, are the prayers of the people of God, and often enough they are the anguished prayers and laments of God's innocent people who suffer apparently without reason. Mark and the other gospels are clearly intending to link Jesus with this long tradition. On the cross Jesus identifies with, enters into, shares, the suffering of all who are persecuted because of their faithfulness to God. This is another aspect of the Old Testament witness to the cross that we need to hold on to.

There is, of course, much more in the Old Testament than I have room for in this chapter. I mentioned the idea of typology at the beginning, though, so I will say something about it again here. Let me take just two stories: Jonah, which Jesus himself uses as a prediction of his death and resurrection, and Abraham setting out to sacrifice Isaac in Genesis 22.

Typology Revisited

Jonah

As I write, we are beginning a preaching series on Jonah at my church. I had to preach the first week, and was looking around at the various commentaries in the university library here. One of them is by a ninth-century monk called Haimo, who takes Jesus' self-identification with Jonah to astonishing lengths. In the first verse of Jonah, for instance, he notices that Jonah is called the 'son of Amittai' and points out that in Hebrew this means 'truth', so Jesus is the 'son of truth'. Jonah is sent to Nineveh, which means 'beautiful', and God created this world to be beautiful, so this is about the incarnation. And so it goes on. The story of Jonah becomes a spiritual parable reminding us of the truths we know about Christ from the New Testament.

I don't think this is what Jesus meant us to do when he spoke of the 'sign of Jonah' in Mt. 12:38–40. Haimo's writing is heartwarming

and inspiring, but if our aim is understanding rather than inspira-
tion, we need to be a bit more measured.

Jesus points to Jonah spending three days in the 'sea monster',
and says that in the same way he will spend three days in the
heart of the earth. It seems a strange image to pick up, but I think
there is something important going on here which it is easy for us
to miss.

We can get so worried about whether it happened or not when
we read about Jonah and the whale (or big fish, or sea monster)
that we can miss what we are actually meant to learn from this bit
of the Bible. Why a big fish, or sea monster? It is, I am sure, a reference to Leviathan, the great sea monster that all the nations
around Israel believed in. Leviathan was the great focus of chaos
and evil (see Is. 27:1; the beasts of Revelation 11–13 probably
recall the Leviathan stories). The Old Testament refers to
Leviathan in two ways: sometimes, as in Isaiah 27:1 or Psalm
74:13–14, God fights against the sea monster and triumphs; at
other points, e.g. in Psalm 104:26 and Genesis 1:21, the sea monsters, too, are God's creatures. The point is the same either way:
the powerful monsters and demons that others believe in are no
match for God: either he defeats them, or they, too, are created by
him for his purposes. (Ps. 104:26 is wonderful: 'you formed
Leviathan to play in the sea' – this great and evil monster, feared
and worshipped by the peoples around, is just God's goldfish,
says the psalmist!)

I think Jesus deliberately says 'sea monster' when referring to
Jonah, in order to bring Leviathan to mind. He retells the story of
Jonah being engulfed by the evil monster that stands against God
as the personification of chaos – and escaping. In the same way
he, too, will face up on the cross to all the powers of sin and death
and hell, meet evil and chaos head on, be swallowed up in death
– and on the third day emerge victorious. When Jesus points us
to Jonah, he is inviting us to understand his cross and resurrection as a decisive victory over all the evil powers that would
oppose God.

Abraham and Isaac

Finally, what of Abraham and Isaac? I commented earlier that it
is difficult not to hear echoes of the gospel story when we read

this strange and troubling narrative. How could God ask Abraham to sacrifice his son? Why should Abraham have to do that? What possible purpose could it serve?

The text is silent – it simply records the heart-rending command.

And Abraham sets out to obey, and ties Isaac on the altar, and raises the knife to kill him – and only then does God intervene, stop the senseless, monstrous, act he apparently demanded.

As preachers we often make this easy comment: God went through with the thing he would not demand of Abraham. It's true, of course, and speaks of the love of God, of the lengths he will go to for us his children, but the 'Why?' question that we surely have to ask when reading Genesis 22 isn't answered. Why does God ask this of Abraham? Why must God go through with it in the end himself?

Søren Kierkegaard, the great Danish philosopher, wrote a book called *Fear and Trembling*, in which he explores the story of Abraham and Isaac. In it, he tells the story time after time, trying to understand how God could command this, and how Abraham could know God had commanded it and that it was not merely a delusion. As Kierkegaard recognised, the God Abraham meets is strange and baffling. He appears and disappears with strange commands and stranger promises, and Abraham tries to respond, to follow, to obey as best he can. Suddenly, Abraham and all his men-folk are commanded to be circumcised – just another bizarre and incomprehensible moment in the story.

Abraham would even dare to question the purposes of God, as he does in Genesis 18:23–33, for example, but he does not presume to understand them.

The Cross in the Old Testament Revisited

Just as in the New Testament, there are several different pictures given to us in the Old to help us understand the cross. Probably, however, the biggest feature portrayed for us in these pictures is mystery.

For example, it is a mystery that hundreds of thousands of animals are slaughtered through the years on the altar of God in obedience to his command, and that somehow their deaths maintain the relationship between Israel and God, covering over sin and fulfilling vows. The reason for God's command is opaque; indeed, his own prophets will later criticise the idea that the blood of bulls and goats means anything to him. Finally, the blood of Jesus will accomplish once and for all what has been endlessly striven for through the sacrificing of bulls and goats, but still we do not know why.

It is a mystery that God's faithful servants suffer unjustly repeatedly, and through Jesus' identification with the anguished psalms of lament we know that in Jesus God suffers with them, but we are given no reason why God does not intervene to stop their suffering.

Finally, a prophet speaks of a mystery – a mysterious servant of the Lord whose unjust suffering will be intended by God, as a sacrifice, as a way of bearing the sins, taking the punishment, of many others. But the prophet himself is astonished at what he tells (Is. 52:15–53:1).

Before and behind it all, Abraham, holding a knife high above the struggling, bound body of his beloved son, terror and confusion in both their eyes, hears once again the strange voice that brought him to that point, but this time it frees him from the terrible burden that it had placed upon him – and God provides a 'lamb' for the offering. And as the blood of the lamb spurts on to the sand of a mountain in Moriah, no one can doubt that blood must be shed, but there is no clear reason why.

And as the blood of the Lamb drips on to the sand of a hill called Calvary, still no one can doubt that blood must be shed. And still, perhaps, there is no clear reason why.

Three

'Come and See the King of Love'

The Cross in the New Testament

Come and see, come and see,
Come and see the King of Love,
See the purple robe and crown of thorns he wears . . .
(Graham Kendrick, 'Come and See' © 1989 Make Way Music)

The Cross at the Heart of the New Testament

The invitation of the New Testament is indeed to 'come and see the King of Love' – to come and see Jesus. And the Jesus the New Testament gospels want us to see is a Jesus who hung on a cross. This might seem a shocking statement, but I believe passionately that it is true.

Some years ago, several people I knew were involved in a Christian musicals society, which existed to perform musical drama with an explicitly Christian message. (Anyone who has had the misfortune to stand near me when a hymn is sung in church will understand that I was never involved!) Once, one of them came back from audition to say he had been given a part in that year's show, which was called *The Virgin and the Passion*. It was actually a performance of two shorter pieces (by Adrian Snell, I think) focussing on both ends of Jesus' life, but we didn't know this, and began to discuss whether this was a good title for a musical on the life of Jesus.

We decided that while it missed out a lot, it was everything the creeds say about the life of Jesus ('. . . was incarnate from the Holy Spirit and the Virgin Mary and was made man. For our sake he was crucified under Pontius Pilate . . .').

The story of the Virgin, telling of the incarnation of God the Son as one of us, and the story of the Passion, telling of his death and resurrection – this is what Christians confess their belief in Sunday by Sunday. It is what they celebrate, too: Christmas and Easter are the highpoints of the year in most churches. Even Handel's great *Messiah* moves straight from birth to death.

But surely this is wrong? Jesus came teaching and healing and living and laughing and loving, and we can't just pretend that all of that is not important, can we?

Well, no – but I think the two moments of the incarnation and the passion, the crib and the cross, are so much more important than the rest, at least for the New Testament, that everything else does have to take second place. If anyone ever forgot the teaching and ministry of Jesus, then that would be wrong, but it is far more wrong to forget the death and resurrection of Jesus, because that is where the focus of the New Testament writings is.

About a hundred years ago the German writer Martin Kähler famously described the four gospels as 'passion narratives with prologues'. Each of them places its focus squarely on the last week of Jesus' life, with everything else leading up to that week, explaining what was happening there.

In Mark, probably the earliest gospel, the story begins with Jesus' baptism. Early Christians could not have read – or written – about baptism without thinking of the death of Jesus – 'are we not baptised into Jesus' death?' (Rom. 6). As soon as Jesus begins his work, there are hints of opposition and conflict, pointing forward to the culmination of opposition to Jesus in the crucifixion (1:45 and 2:7 are examples of this early opposition). Jesus' first prediction of his coming death is as early as 2:20, and the middle section of the gospel is punctuated by predictions of the suffering and death of Jesus (8:31; 9:31; 10:33). The way of discipleship is explicitly identified with the cross of Jesus, at an important moment in the narrative (8:34–38). Even the relative lack of a resurrection narrative in the shortest ending of Mark (ending at 16:8, which is probably the original version) makes the point: it is a death that is the focus of this story, a death that is followed by a resurrection, to be sure, but nonetheless, the focus is squarely on cross and death.

The same is true of the other three gospels, in different ways. Most of the teaching and miracles in Luke are arranged around

the final journey of Jesus to Jerusalem. The big theme of
Matthew's presentation is the developing conflict between Jesus
and the leaders of Israel, which reaches an apparently decisive
end when, very suddenly, the wavering crowds and the apparently faithful disciples turn against Jesus, and he dies alone. Only
the mighty act of God can reverse this death.

John's Gospel is often divided into the 'book of signs' (chapters 2–12, recording the seven 'signs', or miracles, that John tells
us about) and the 'book of the passion' (chapters 13–20).
However, John's own account of his purpose suggests that the
whole gospel is a 'book of signs' (20:30–31), and the death of
Jesus is the most important sign of the book. The predictions
and interpretations of the suffering of Jesus begin in 1:29 and
2:19 and continue throughout the first half of the book: if
Christ's death is the last and greatest of the signs, the signs
themselves point towards that death. The moment of Jesus' glorification is identified squarely with his death on the cross. A
more profound focus on the cross within the narrative is difficult to imagine.

For a final piece of evidence, consider Paul's summary of what
was of 'first importance' in the gospel he preached, that formed
the foundation of his churches: 'In the foremost place, I handed
on to you the tradition which I had received, that Christ died for
our sins, according to the Scriptures. And that he was buried.
And that he rose again on the third day, according to the
Scriptures . . .' (1 Cor. 15:3–4).

If the creeds and the worship of the church move straight from
incarnation to passion, by doing that they capture a biblical perspective on the gospel story. *The Virgin and the Passion?* Yes. That
is not quite the whole story, but it is the biblical emphasis in the
story of Jesus.

If the New Testament focuses on the cross of Jesus, how do we
understand what is going on there?

When Mel Gibson released his shockingly graphic and powerful meditation on the suffering and death of Jesus, *The Passion of
the Christ*, many churches realised that this was a moment of
opportunity, but that the film itself was inadequate. It gave the
(non-Christian) viewer no framework for understanding why
Jesus suffered and died like this. So churches handed out tracts,

and gave talks and seminars, containing stories and illustrations to try to explain to people the meaning of this brutal death.

The Bible does the same thing: it offers pictures, stories, images which help us to understand why Jesus died and what his death did for us. I want to look at some of these pictures now.

I have picked out eight; this is not all of the different pictures found in the New Testament, certainly, and they may not even be the eight most important ones, but they do give something of the range of ideas offered.

One comment on these pictures: you sometimes hear people say that it was Paul and others who tried to make the death of Jesus symbolic or important; that the gospels, and Jesus' own words, did not. This is just not true, and I have deliberately illustrated every single one of these pictures with at least one quote from the gospels.

Sacrifice

At the beginning of the fourth gospel, John the Baptist points to Jesus and declares, 'See, the lamb of God!' At the end of that gospel, notoriously, Jesus is apparently killed a day earlier than in the other three gospels. There are ways of explaining this disagreement, which commentaries discuss, but the effect of it is striking: Jesus in John's Gospel is nailed to the cross at the very time the Passover lambs were being sacrificed. Centuries earlier, Isaiah had prophesied about a 'Servant of the Lord' who would be 'led like a lamb to the slaughter', 'taken away by a miscarriage of justice', and whose 'life would be made an offering for sin' (Is. 53:7–10). Peter applies Isaiah's prophecy to the death of Jesus in his first letter (1 Pet. 2:24).

All this recalls the sacrifices commanded by God in the Old Testament law, by which the sin and guilt of Israel would be covered over. Jesus is the one great sacrifice, whose blood 'can make the foulest clean', whose death makes atonement once for all, for the whole world.

The blood of Passover lamb was smeared around the doors of the houses of God's people, so that the avenging angel of God, bringing terrible judgement to the earth, would 'pass over' them (Ex. 12). Paul picks up this idea of Christ as the Passover lamb in 1 Corinthians 5:7.

The place where we find the most sustained witness to the idea that Jesus died as a sacrifice to God, however, is in the book of Hebrews. Picking up passage after passage of Old Testament imagery, the writer recalls that sacrifice was given to the people so that the blood, the life, of the sacrificed animal could be used for 'making atonement' on the altar (Lev. 17:11), and boldly asserts that 'without the shedding of blood there is no forgiveness' (Heb. 9:22). But, he then says, Jesus offers the one perfect sacrifice that brings an end to all that had come before, offering 'for all time a single sacrifice for sins' (Heb. 10:12).

We might want to ask how this works – how does sacrifice turn away God's wrath, and bring forgiveness for sin?

The simple answer is that the Bible does not tell us. As we saw, the closest we get is in Leviticus 17:11, which is difficult to translate, but links 'life' with 'blood' in making atonement.

I believe, however, that all the sacrifices of the Old Testament were a preparation for the coming of Jesus, so that there was a ready way of picturing, explaining, what he came to do. In his death our sins are forgiven and we are cleansed from uncleanness. Through his death our relationship with God is renewed and restored. In his death we find life, forgiveness, hope.

Victory

The image of Jesus the Lamb carries forward into the last book of the New Testament, Revelation. But it appears there in a surprising way.

John has been granted a vision of heaven, and sees a scroll 'written on the inside and outside, and sealed with seven seals' (Rev. 5:1). John – and his readers – would have known all about this scroll. It is a standard symbol representing all the judgements of God that are to fall upon the earth. John sees this during his exile on Patmos and knows that if only that scroll could be opened, then his suffering, oppressed people would be set free, the churches vindicated, the name of Jesus glorified, the kingdom of God ushered in. It was all wrapped up in the scroll.

Yet 'no one in heaven or on earth or under the earth was able to open the scroll . . .' (5:3). No one could help! And so, in the middle of the throne room of heaven, John bursts out crying.

But then, in Revelation 5:5, John is told to look at 'the Lion of the tribe of Judah' who 'has conquered, so that he can open the scroll . . .' And so he looks – 'and I saw a Lamb, bearing the marks of slaughter' (5:6).

This is only one of several places in Revelation where John is told to look at one thing and then sees something completely different. In every case it happens to sharpen the contrast between what we would all have expected (if we were used to reading books like Revelation), and what actually occurs. In this particular place we all expect to see a divine conqueror, and we do – but the conqueror bears the marks of slaughter.

The New Testament pictures Jesus' death and resurrection as a victory over the evil powers of sin and death and hell in several places. In Colossians 2:15 we read of Jesus leading a procession of triumph, as the ancient Roman emperors did to celebrate their military conquests. This theme is perhaps most powerfully developed in 1 Corinthians 15, which culminates in the great shout of Easter triumph, 'Death is swallowed up in victory!' Jesus speaks of a battle with the powers of evil more than once in the gospels as well. The 'strong man' needs to be overcome and bound before those he holds captive can be set free (Mt. 12:29; see also Lk. 13:16).

The victory, however, is a strange one: it is won as Jesus dies. It would have been easier to see the victory at the resurrection only, but that is not the way Revelation and Colossians and other texts tell the story. In some mysterious way, Jesus conquers all by dying and rising. This needs to be a part, too, of any biblical account of what Jesus was doing on the cross.

Ransom

'The Son of Man came not to be served, but to serve . . .' So said Jesus to followers who sought positions of power and authority in his kingdom – but he went on to add, 'and give his life as a ransom for many' (Mk 10:45 and Mt. 20:28). This again seems to recall Isaiah 52:13–53:12, with its picture of the Servant of the Lord suffering and dying for his people.

A ransom is a price paid to set someone free. Today the word only really gets used about kidnap victims, but it used to be a lot more common. In medieval Europe, one of the standard consequences of a battle was the capture of some of the troops and leaders of the los-ing side. They would often be cared for very well, in the hope that their people might be forced into paying a ransom to release them. Taxation began in Scotland to raise the ransom paid to England for the release of King James I; England had earlier suffered in trying to raise the ransom to rescue King Richard after the Crusades (remem-ber all those tales of Robin Hood?).

In the Bible *ransom* is used more than once to describe the price that must be paid to set someone free from their sins and from the threat of hell. Job 33:24 comes in the middle of a long passage where Elihu imagines the fate of people who have sinned (v. 27), who need 'a mediator' who can say, 'Deliver him from the Pit, for I have found a ransom' (v. 24). Psalm 49 asks what ransom price could possibly be enough for a person's life (vv. 5–9), using this to mock those who trust in their wealth rather than God. The psalmist goes on to announce that 'God will ransom my soul from the power of the Pit – he will receive me' (v. 15). When Jesus said he would give his life 'as a ransom for many', this notion of paying the unimaginably costly price necessary to rescue human-ity must be what he meant.

Who was the ransom paid to? As we will see in chapter four, the church struggled with that question, and the Bible does not really answer it, but the general picture is clear: Jesus, by dying, pays a ransom to set us free.

Healing and salvation

'You will call him by the name Jesus because he will save his peo-ple from their sins,' says the angel to Joseph in those well-known words in Matthew 1:21. The Greek word here translated save can also mean 'heal' (as in James 5:15: 'the faithful prayer will heal the sick person', where the same word is used).

But we need to ask: What are we saved from, or healed of?

The angel in Matthew says 'from their sins', which might be shorthand for 'from the guilt of their sins', but is not necessarily that – it might also mean that we are saved or delivered from, or healed of, the sins that drag us down; set free to be holy.

In the Old Testament, salvation usually refers to physical deliv-erance of God's people from their enemies, often in a military way (Judg. 3:31 and 8:22, for example), but also from disaster or disease (Ps. 107:19). Elsewhere in the New Testament we are saved from God's wrath (Rom. 5:9), from final judgement and hell (1 Cor. 5:5), and from death (James 5:20), as well as from sickness (Jas. 5:15 again).

We could try to find a way of putting all these different images together, tracing the links between God's wrath and disease and disaster and death and judgement and hell. And if we were to try to understand the wonders of what Jesus did on the cross for us we would probably need to do this. But the New Testament doesn't do it, and we need to take that fact seriously – salvation and healing are another set of images that are employed, not in a careful logical way, but in an attempt to grab hold of and describe the wonderful truth of what God has done in Jesus.

Reconciliation

'Jesus cried again, loudly, and breathed his last breath. Right at that moment, the curtain of the temple was torn in two from top to bottom' (Mt. 27:50–51; see also Mk 15:37–38). The Jewish temple had two curtains, both of which were symbolic barriers. The first separated the Court of the Gentiles (everyone who wasn't Jewish) from the Court of the Jews. Gentiles could come that far, but no further. They were not God's chosen people, and so they were prevented from coming even close to the place at the heart of the temple where God was present on Earth.

It probably wasn't this first curtain that was torn when Jesus died, but if it had been, it would have been deeply significant, as Paul tells us again and again that in dying Jesus broke down the old barriers that prevented non-Jews from any share in the promises God made to his people. In Ephesians 2 we are told that Gentiles were 'strangers to the covenants of promise, without hope, and without God in the world' (v. 12), but Jesus 'through the cross' (v. 16) 'has smashed the wall that divided' (v. 14). Whether this curtain was meant or not, there is a real 'horizontal' reconciliation achieved by the cross, according to the New Testament, a bringing together of people across traditional dividing lines that Paul witnesses to in Galatians 3:28.

On April 10, 1998, Good Friday that year, I was watching the big Easter film on TV in the afternoon. It was, yet again, *Ben Hur*. As the story moved to its climax, and we had the long, lingering shot of the crosses of Jesus and the two thieves on the hill from a distance, a newsflash started scrolling across the bottom of the screen telling us that an agreement had been reached in Stormont to bring an end to the decades of terrorism and oppression in Northern Ireland. The news was expected, of course (and the progress of the agreement has been troubled enough since), but that TV screen was a powerful image, still, of the reconciliation that the cross does and should bring about between human enemies – the meaning of one of the curtains in the temple.

The other curtain in the temple was an even more significant barrier, however. It separated the Holy Place from the Most Holy Place. The Holy Place contained the altar, the place where the priests could come to present the offerings of the people to God. Behind that, though, in the Most Holy Place, God himself was present with his people. Once each year the high priest was permitted to enter through that curtain, and no one else could ever go.

This is all described in Hebrews 9:2–7. God dwelt with his people in the temple, yes, but the curtain separated him from them, forbidding access, proclaiming his otherness. The writer to the Hebrews suggests that this was the curtain that was torn (Heb. 6:19 and 10:19–20) – not only did the cross break down the barriers between different human beings, it also broke down the barrier that separated us from God: What was this barrier?

Hebrews makes it clear that the issue is human sin (e.g. 9:7, 9, 12.). Adam and Eve, in the Garden, were permitted free conversation with God until they sinned; then, even before God cast out them out of the Garden, they were ashamed and afraid of meeting him (Gen. 3:8). The angel with the flaming sword (Gen. 3:24) and our own shame and guilt combine to prevent humanity coming near to God. In talking about the cross as an act of reconciliation, or in recalling the torn curtain, we are saying simply, but profoundly, that through Jesus' death we are reconciled to God; our relationship with God is restored. This picture doesn't tell us how Jesus' death does this for us, but it promises us that this is the case.

Revelation

As Jesus dies in Mark's account, the centurion looking on sees the way Jesus dies and announces: 'Surely this man was God's Son!' (Mk 15:39).

This claim is enormously significant for Mark: he has announced that his gospel is about 'Jesus Christ, God's Son' (Mk 1:1), but the only people in the entire gospel who 'get it', who confess that Jesus is the Son of God, are the demons who recognise him already (Mk 3:11), and this centurion who watches him die. It is Jesus' death on the cross that reveals who he is. At the beginning of 1 Corinthians, in the face of demands for clever wisdom or miraculous signs, Paul insists that it is the cross of Christ – not his life in general, not the resurrection, but the cross of Christ – that reveals the power and the wisdom of God (1 Cor. 1:22–24). In 1 John 4:9–10, the coming of Christ, and the death of Christ on the cross, together reveal God's love. The cross is an act of revelation.

Of course, God reveals himself in other ways too. But consider the list above: Jesus' identity; God's wisdom, power, and love. These are central things. Martin Luther, the German Reformer, claimed that we did not know God at all unless we knew him through the cross. When we make a list of the New Testament images of what the cross does, revelation has to be on it.

New covenant

Covenant is a big idea in the Bible: God repeatedly made covenants with his people, promising to be their God, and instructing them how to live in the light of that promise (e.g. Gen. 6:18, 15:18; Ex. 34:10; 2 Sam. 23:5; 2 Kgs 11:7).

John has Jesus crucified just as the Passover lambs are being slaughtered; the other three gospels, by contrast, have him eating a Passover meal – the last supper – with his disciples. During that meal, Jesus took bread and wine, blessed them, and gave them to his followers. The bread, he said, was his body (Luke adds 'broken for you'); the wine was his blood, the *new* covenant, poured out for many (Matthew adds 'for the forgiveness of sins'). Thus Jesus began a new covenant, renewing and extending God's Old Testament promise.

But every covenant, according to Hebrews (9:18), demanded the shedding of blood to seal it, and *blood of the covenant* is a recurring phrase in Scripture, in both Testaments (e.g. Ex. 24:8; Zech. 9:11). So when Jesus, looking forward towards the cross, speaks of the cup he offers his followers as a 'new covenant in my blood', it is a recurring scriptural theme he is picking up. Through his death on the cross, Jesus establishes a new covenant for us. Why does a covenant need to be sealed in blood? Once again we have to say the Scriptures are not clear. Hebrews 9 tries to defend the principle on the basis of a rather odd argument about wills (or 'testaments', which is the translation of the same word that is also translated *covenants*) not becoming effective until after a death, but this looks more like a preacher's illustration than a logical explanation of the point to me. Whatever . . . it is the case that every covenant begins with death, with sacrifice; and Jesus' new covenant is no different.

Justification

When Nicodemus, a respectable religious scholar, came to see Jesus by night, Jesus responded to his questions with perhaps the most famous verse in the Bible: 'God so loved the world that he gave his one and only Son, so that whoever believes in him might not perish, but have eternal life' (Jn 3:16). The gift of life here is, however, closely linked to the cross. Jesus has already talked about being 'lifted up' just as Moses 'lifted up the snake in the wilderness' (Jn 3:14). This is a reference to Numbers 21:4–9, where the people of Israel in the wilderness are being punished by a plague of snakes; they ask Moses to pray for them, which Moses does, and God tells him to make a model snake out of bronze and put it on a pole, and after that anyone bitten by a snake is healed when he or she looks at the bronze snake on the pole. Jesus borrows the story as an image of the salvation he will win for God's people.

Once again, the Old Testament story gives no hint as to why this should work, other than God's promise that it will.

Jesus has a bit more than that to say, however: he speaks of the judgement and condemnation which God might bring on the world (Jn 3:17–18), which is turned away by belief in Jesus – more specifically belief in the cross of Jesus, given the use of the Numbers story earlier. The cross averts judgement.

This becomes a very big theme in Paul. In Romans 3:21–26, for instance, he works out at some length how judgement and condemnation are avoided, and righteousness achieved and received, through the cross of Jesus.

There is a fairly major change of view going on amongst Pauline scholars at the moment. Many are questioning whether Paul's writings are really all about universal guilt before the implacable law of God (as Protestants since the Reformation have traditionally understood Paul). Instead, they suggest, it is much more about how God's covenant with Israel can be opened up to all nations without their having to keep every aspect of the Jewish ceremonial law (circumcision, for example). This becomes a debate about the meaning of words like *justified* and *righteous* (and indeed *sin* and *guilt*). Are these really legal terms, to do with guilt and innocence, as we have traditionally understood them before God, or are they far more about being and living within God's covenant?

This is not the place to go into the argument, but it seems to me that the answer is going to be more 'both and' than 'either or'.

In Galatians, for example, the question at the heart of things seems to be: 'Do Christians need to be circumcised?' That is clearly a question about covenant markers, and the 'law' in Galatians should be understood in that way.

In Romans, however, while Paul is definitely interested in Jewish-Gentile relations (Rom. 9–11 is all about that!), a passage like Romans 3:9–18, which gives a litany of moral failures committed by Jew and Gentile alike, surely cannot be read as simply a question of badges of God's covenant people. Whether part of God's ancient people or not, 'there is no distinction, as all have sinned and missed God's glory' (Rom. 3:23); and, equally, 'all are now justified . . . by the redemption that is in Christ Jesus, whom God presented as a sacrifice of atonement by his blood' (Rom. 3:24–25). The train of thought here surely demands that some notion of moral failure and responsibility is in view, even if we want to resist reading that in terms of the modern law court.

What all this Says About the Place of the Cross

What does all this tell us? Three things, I think:

1. The New Testament writers did focus on the cross. Even when it would have been easy to discuss a theme without much

mention of the cross (as, for example, victory), they would not. The focus is constant – in the gospel writers, in Paul, in the other letters, and in Revelation.

2. In trying to understand, explain, or apply the message of the cross, the New Testament uses many different images. These images are not related in any obvious or organised way within the New Testament itself.

3. Many of the images are partial or incomplete. For example, Jesus' death can be described as the payment of a ransom, without any reflection on who receives the payment. The shocking (to a modern Western mind at least) assumption that the founding of a new covenant requires the shedding of blood can be stated with little or no defence or discussion. A word like 'save' can be used in several different ways, without any need to work out how they relate.

Given this, let me end the chapter with two comments about the general argument of the book.

First, I have already said that I will be arguing that the best way to think about the cross is to use many, complementary, models or stories of salvation that hint at and point towards the indescribable truth at the heart of the matter. It seems clear that this is what the New Testament writers did.

Second, what of penal substitution? Is it taught in the New Testament? We need to be careful here. There is, as far as I can see, no clearly worked out doctrine of atonement in the New Testament. Instead, there is only the raw material out of which we may and must attempt to construct such a doctrine. And this shouldn't surprise us: most of the central beliefs of Christianity are built on the foundations of the Scriptures, rather than read straight out of them. For example, other than a dubious verse in 1 John 4:7, which is almost certainly a later addition to the text by a zealous Christian scribe, God's being as Trinity is not taught directly anywhere in Scripture, but it is unquestionably a biblical doctrine.

How to View Jesus

The New Testament invites us to view Jesus in at least three ways: as our *example*, as our *representative*, and as our *substitute*.

Imitating the attitudes and actions of Christ, even as he offers himself on the cross, is clearly a biblical theme (e.g. Phil. 2:1–8). Christ is an example for us.

At other times, Christ is pictured as acting as our representative. Representatives act on others' behalf, and there is a sense in which their acts are our acts; for example, a head of state can declare war or peace, and does so on behalf of everyone in the country. In Romans 6, Paul speaks of being 'baptized into Christ's death', telling us that 'we have died with Christ'. What Jesus did, he did on behalf of us all, and we were included in that – he was our representative.

Finally, Jesus is sometimes pictured as our substitute: he does things so that we don't have to. In Galatians 3:13 we read that 'Christ redeemed us from the curse of the law by becoming a curse for us.' He took the curse on himself so that we would no longer have to bear it. Unquestionably, there is material in the Bible that invites us to think of the atonement in substitutionary terms.

How about 'penal' terms?

There are perhaps two problems with this. The first is the claim that current Western understandings of criminal justice differ markedly from biblical ones.

This is no doubt true, but equally they are not totally different. People sometimes claim that a judge in Israel was not there to punish the offender, but to restore justice. There might be some truth in that, but it is surely an oversimplification: the punishment, by fines or death, of thieves and murderers is hardly absent from either biblical law codes or biblical history. We need to be conscious that our courts were not their courts, and careful whenever we draw the analogy, but that does not of itself prevent us from talking in penal terms about the atonement if the Bible uses the penal language of judgement and guilt.

Which raises the second problem: Does it?

I mentioned above the debate about how these words are used in Paul in particular. I also indicated some reasons for believing that the words retained some sort of moral or ethical content.

Much of the language about the atonement in the New Testament could be understood in penal substitutionary terms if we had good reason to do so, but equally could be understood in other terms. When we read of Jesus 'redeeming' us, or 'paying the price' for our sin, if we already know from somewhere else that penal substitution is the right way to understand the atonement, then we can read these as different ways of describing penal substitution. When you look at writers arguing that penal substitution is the right way to understand the cross in the Bible, this seems to be what a lot of them do.

It might be right, but the New Testament language does not, as far as I can see, *demand* to be read that way, and there is value (particularly, perhaps, in the face of controversy) in pausing with the many different images the New Testament does use, and refusing to interpret them too quickly into saying something else.

The closest I can find to a straightforward teaching of penal substitution in the New Testament is this text from Colossians: 'God made you alive, along with Christ, when he forgave us all our sins, erasing the record that stood against us, with its legal demands. He set this aside by nailing it to the cross.' (Col. 2:13–14). What was nailed to the cross? Jesus, of course. Here, Jesus carries or bears – or just simply *is* – the legal charge sheet that we faced.

The verse is not quite full-blown penal substitution: the charge sheet is here 'erased' and 'set aside' – there is no explicit statement of Jesus bearing the penalty of our sins. But the New Testament, here and elsewhere, at least allows us, and perhaps invites us, to begin to think in that direction to see if it will help us to understand how we are washed and saved by the death of the King of Love.

Four

'Tell me the Old, Old Story'

The Cross in Christian History

Tell me the story slowly,
That I may take it in –
That wonderful redemption,
God's remedy for sin.

(Katherine Hankey, 'Tell me the Old, Old Story')

Keeping the Cross Central

I don't know about other denominations, or other countries, but many British Baptist churches these days are getting rid of their pulpits and replacing them with moveable lecterns. Before we had radio mikes, and loop systems to help people with hearing problems, raised pulpits were important – they helped a preacher to be heard. These days pulpits do tend to get in the way of using the church in all the ways we want to use it, and they put a very unhelpful barrier between the preacher and the congregation, so I am not sad to see them go.

When I have preached in churches that still had their old pulpits, however, I have noticed two very common features: a clock set into the wood so that the preacher can put his or her Bible on it and not be distracted by it; and a text carved into the wood where only the preacher can see it, which is almost always the same: 'Sir, we would see Jesus!' (Jn. 12:21, KJV)

Advice from wise congregations to foolish preachers, perhaps, who might be tempted to talk about something else – politics, or current affairs, or moral issues. I once heard the great missionary

Lesslie Newbigin preach, right towards the end of his life, addressing a group of young ministers. He spent twenty-eight minutes telling us all about these sorts of things that we might be tempted to do as ministers, and that we shouldn't, and then asked very simply, 'So what should you be doing?' and, with a smile that lit up the whole room, answered his own question: 'Tell them about Jesus – tell them about the wonderful thing that God has done!' And then he stopped. Whenever I am given the chance to speak in theological colleges, I take the same message, preaching always on Paul's assertion about his own ministry: 'We preach Christ, and him crucified.'

From the days of Paul until now, people have given themselves to Jesus, and churches have started and grown, because preachers, evangelists, and other Christians were true to that example.

The New Testament period fades into Christian history about fifty years after the ascension of Jesus: the latest of the New Testament books were being written sometime around then, probably, and the earliest Christian writings we have that aren't in the Bible come from about the same period. We also have all sorts of other evidence about those very early churches: letters from Roman governors asking what to do about the Christians; Jewish or Roman historians who mention Jesus and his followers; scraps of copies of this or that biblical book; graffiti in caves where people met for worship – all sorts of bits and pieces. In all of this, one thing stands out: the story of Jesus, crucified and risen, is right at the heart of everything that is going on.

Perhaps the most powerful evidence of the centrality of the cross is in the very earliest Christian art, which consists of fairly crude decorations in copies of biblical books. From remarkably early on, there are references to the cross. The most famous, perhaps, is the 'Chi-rho' symbol, where the name of Christ is decorated with a cross. The Greek letter Chi, the first letter of *Christ*, looks rather like our letter X, but in Christian manuscripts it was turned around slightly, to something like † – a cross. Even earlier than this, though, even in the earliest Christian writings we have, the Greek word for *cross* had been decorated with a letter-symbol looking like a man on a cross. From the first, Christ was not known apart from his cross. These first Christians looked to the cross of Christ as their salvation and reason for living and suffering all that they did.

How did they understand that salvation, though? If the cross made all the difference, *how* did it make that difference?

People sometimes say that no one ever asked that question until a thousand years after the birth of Christianity. That has a germ of truth in it, in that the first person to write a book asking the simple question: 'How do Christ's life and death and resurrection save us?' was probably St Anselm sometime in the 1090s. Even Anselm, however, knew about all sorts of other theories, and wrote to oppose them. Many writers had offered answers to the question, but they'd done it almost in passing, a side note when they were really writing about something else, and no one had really collected the various answers and attempted to see if they were biblical and if they made any sense until Anselm tried to do so.

It is certainly true, of course, as I said in the first chapter, that Christian people have always cared more about standing under the cross than understanding it. Being saved by Jesus is what matters, far more than understanding how he did it. When my computer crashes, I want help from someone who can get my documents back for me; I don't care very much about whether I understand how he or she did it. Jesus saves us from all the powers of sin and death and hell – that is what matters; *how* he does it is far, far less important.

In the earliest arguments about Christian theology we actually find that people do not argue about redemption or salvation. They assume it, and argue from it.

The classic example is perhaps St Gregory of Nazianzus. Gregory was one of the so-called Cappadocian Fathers, a group of church leaders who lived and worked in Cappadocia, a Roman province in what is now Turkey, around 350–400 AD and who helped settle orthodox Christian theology about the Trinity.

Gregory also wrote about one Apollinarius, who was trying to understand how the incarnation worked. Apollinarius had suggested that human beings were made up of three parts: a body, a soul and a spirit, and that Jesus of Nazareth had a human body and a human soul, but the divine Son took the place of his spirit. This, of course, makes Jesus less than fully human. One of Gregory's arguments against this began from the experience of salvation. We are saved through Jesus, he claimed, and so if there is any part of our humanity that Jesus didn't share, that part could not be saved. Jesus had to be fully human, just as human as you or me, or he could not save us. As Gregory famously put it: 'That which he did not assume he could not heal.' He was arguing *from* a belief in salvation through Jesus, not *for* such a belief.

There are three significant ways of describing how Jesus Christ has saved us that were current in Gregory's day. They were not in competition, and many writers slipped from one to another quite naturally and unconsciously. (I've mentioned two of them before, but I develop the ideas and arguments more fully here.)

As a ransom

The first was a development of the biblical idea of ransom – that Jesus' death somehow pays the ransom that needed to be paid to set us free. But the question is: Who was the ransom paid to?

Some thought it was paid to the devil. Through Adam and Eve's sin, the devil acquired rights over them and all other human beings. Just as slaves belong to this or that owner, and can only be set free by someone buying them from that owner, we belonged to the devil until Jesus gave his life to the devil as a payment that bought freedom for the rest of us.

This is simple and neat, but other people asked whether it was really right to believe that the devil had rights that God had to respect. Surely God just defeats Satan – he doesn't have to bargain with him?

There are ways of answering the question, 'Who was the ransom paid to?'

In one of the earliest discussions of the atonement, St Irenaeus of Lyons (who tells us at one point that his own teacher, Polycarp, was taught by the gospel writer John) emphasises the justice of God, who will not act to conquer, but deals rightly with all, even the devil. St Augustine of Hippo, the greatest of the Western church fathers, made a similar point: the devil's rights over us were established justly, so God had to respect them.

Augustine goes on, however, to introduce an unhappy, but fairly common, element of these ransom theories: the idea that God deceived the devil. Because Jesus had not sinned, the devil had no rights over Jesus, and so the death of Jesus involved the devil in taking something that wasn't his. The most grotesque version of this 'deception' idea comes in another of the Cappadocian fathers, St Gregory of Nyssa, who used the image of a fish hook concealed under tempting bait: the devil saw the holy humanity of Jesus and wanted to destroy him, but didn't notice the hidden deity, was snared into taking the life of the incarnate Son, and so accepted the ransom that would free all humanity, without intending to.

This argument can be rejected outright. Quite apart from the problems of the idea of God acting deceptively, the gospels are clear on the idea that demons and other powers of darkness are well aware of who Jesus is – indeed far more so than all the human people he meets!

There is something interesting in all of this, however: several writers, perhaps drawing on the image of God's relationship with the devil in Job 1–2, suggest that the 'right' which the devil had over us as a result of Adam's sin was the right to inflict the punishment of death, decreed by God in Genesis 3:19. St John Chrysostom, a great fourth-century preacher, talks like this, as do several Western theologians: Augustine of Hippo (again); Pope Leo the Great; St Ambrose; and Rufinus. When Anselm came to write his book, this idea was common enough for him to pause to argue against it.

There are problems, then, with understanding the death of Jesus as a ransom paid to the devil. But could we perhaps understand all the biblical talk about the death of Jesus being a ransom paid to God?

St Gregory of Nazianzus, whom we have already met, thought it was ridiculous for the ransom to be offered to the devil, calling the devil a 'thief' and a 'tyrant' and insisting that he can have no rights. However, since Jesus himself talked of his death as a ransom, we cannot get away from that idea. Therefore, says Gregory, the ransom must be paid to God.

Gregory is well aware of the problems with this: it is not God who holds us in bondage, so no ransom is due to him; and he finds the notion that God could want the sacrifice of his Son, when he turned away Abraham's offer of Isaac, very difficult. He ends his argument by saying, effectively, that if the death of Christ was a ransom, and it cannot have been paid to the devil, we must believe it was paid to God, despite the difficulties.

As a conquest of the evil powers

A second idea of atonement used very widely in the early church
was that Christ's work was a battle with, and conquest of, the evil
powers. Again, the idea is already present in the Bible, as we have
seen.

Many of the writers who talk about the death of Jesus as a ransom also talk about the work of Jesus in terms of victory. Human
beings are enslaved by evil powers: the devil; demons; the 'prin-
cipalities and powers' that rule over this world; even death itself.
Jesus in his life and death meets these evil powers head on and
wins a decisive victory over them. Of course, the way in which
Jesus conquers is surprising: he does not do it by overwhelming
military force ('Could I not ask my Father, and he would send me
more than twelve legions of angels?' – Mt. 26:53), but instead he
lets sin and death and hell do their worst to him – and then
emerges unscathed, thus disempowering these enemies of
humanity.

As with the ransom theory, this way of thinking is based on a
worldview which had an acute sense of the reality of evil spiritual powers; if this seems strange to modern Western minds, we
perhaps need to recall that it is not a reality described only in the
New Testament – the growing churches of the global south often
emphasise the importance of ministries of exorcism and the like.

As a restoration of our humanness

The third common account of atonement we find in these early
years is even more foreign to modern Westerners' normal ways of
thinking. It is usually called the 'physical theory', but that is
already potentially misleading: *physical* here has nothing to do
with athletics or exercise, or even bodies; it comes from the Greek
physis, which means 'nature', as in *human nature*.

Many early Christians believed that all human beings shared
in something real which we can call 'human nature', and that this
is what made them human. (Plato and other Greek philosophers
had taught this.) When Adam and Eve fell, this human nature
was corrupted, cursed and damaged. So we are all inevitably corrupted, cursed and damaged by the fall, because we are all connected to this 'human nature'. By becoming human, God the Son

heals and restores this human nature and so heals and restores us all.

This is probably a very strange idea to most of us, but it might help to think of it like this: I am British – I was born in Britain (in Derbyshire) and I live in Britain (in Fife). Things can happen which affect the whole of Britain – for example, another country declares war on Britain; Parliament passes a law that is binding in Britain; whatever . . . These things affect me because I am a part of a bigger whole called Britain.

This is not an exact picture of what I am talking about, since on one hand, for example, my non-British friends who happen to live here also have to obey laws passed by the British parliament despite not being British; and, on the other, I as a Briton could march with a banner or wear a badge proclaiming 'Not in my name!' and so try to disassociate myself from a war that Britain is fighting, but the analogy might convey some idea of what is involved in the concept we're looking at.

This way of thinking about the atonement puts the focus on Christmas rather than on Easter: it is the incarnation that saves us, not the passion. We would need, then, to ask why Jesus lived and died as he did. (Indeed, in one very interesting version of this theory, St Irenaeus argues that Jesus had to relive every part of human life as it should have been lived, and so claims that Jesus must have been crucified in old age, not aged thirty-three.)

As with every explanation of the atonement, there are problems if we think this is a complete answer to the question, 'How does Jesus save us?', but it was one important way of talking about the atonement in the early church.

Other Pictures

Alongside these three major ideas there are many other interesting hints or idiosyncratic ideas in the first thousand years of Christianity.

The language of medicine is fairly common, for example, and often connected to a high doctrine of the sacraments: eating the body and drinking the blood of Christ in the communion service heals us of our sin.

Sacrificial language is everywhere, although very rarely worked up into any sort of explanation of how Jesus saves us. We also find hints that Christ's death is an example to inspire us to heights of self-sacrificial love.

Early Christian Thinkers

St John of Damascus, sometimes called the last of the church fathers, lived in the eighth century, and his great genius lay in pulling together much of the theology that had gone before. We might, therefore, take his work as a summing up of the Greek tradition from the earlier centuries.

His main account of salvation is 'physicalist': Jesus transforms human nature through the incarnation. When he speaks of the cross, however, he sees it in two main ways: he uses language of sacrifice to describe the cross, and he understands the effects of the cross as the gifts given in baptism, which he sees as a true washing away of sin.

What of penal substitution? Is there any hint of this way of talking about the atonement in these early Christian thinkers?

I have indicated already that one (fairly common) form of the ransom theory saw the devil as having the right to punish humanity, a right which was lost when it was exercised improperly on Christ. I don't think this really counts as penal substitution, although it is perhaps a way of understanding the cross that is headed in the same direction.

St Athanasius comes closer in one or two passing references, where he sees a judgement of law which Christ takes on himself so that we do not have to suffer it.

The greatest preacher of the early church, St John Chrysostom, tells a parable at one point about a king who 'transfers' the death and punishment due to a criminal onto his son, which sounds very like penal substitution.

However, there is one early writer who teaches penal substitution clearly and unambiguously – not as his only account of how Christ saves us, but as one significant answer to that question: Gregory the Great (who was elected Pope in 590, aged about fifty, and died in 604). He puts aside all notions of the devil's rights and teaches plainly that the punishment for human sin is death, and that the Father inflicted this punishment on Christ (who bore it willingly) so that we might be freed from it.

I have not found any evidence that Gregory's thoughts were particularly influential, however, and five centuries later, when Anselm set out to change what his fellow Christians believed about atonement, he took the earlier ransom theories as the ones that needed to be argued against.

Anselm

St Anselm (1033–1109) was appointed Archbishop of Canterbury in 1093. He had previously been Abbot of a Monastery in Bec (in northern France), and his role as Archbishop included leading the community of monks attached to the cathedral. Unquestionably a great scholar, Anselm wrote on many subjects, often, it seems, with the intention of clearing up difficulties his monks had raised. His book on the atonement, *Cur Deus Homo* ('The Reason for the God-man') is an imaginary conversation with one of these monks, who keeps asking him questions about the cross, which Anselm answers and so explains his ideas. The monk is called Boso (and sometimes lives up to the name!).

Anselm angrily rejects the idea that the cross is about a ransom paid to the devil. Like Gregory of Nazianzus, he believes that the devil has no rights. Boso therefore suggests that God could simply forgive us and welcome us into heaven without any need for any help from Christ. Anselm's response has become famous: 'You have not yet understood how serious a thing sin is' – sin, even the slightest sin, is an act of rebellion against God.

We need to understand how European society worked in Anselm's day to understand what he meant by this.

In Anselm's feudal society, obedience and honour were owed by social inferiors (vassals) to social superiors (lieges): a serf owed obedience to his landlord, a knight to his baron, the baron to the earl, the earl to the king, and so on. (In tangible terms, this might involve a regular payment of money – a form of tax; or the vassal might have to fight a war, and to bring many of his own vassals to fight with him if the liege demanded it.) If the obedience and honour owed were not given, the offence was considered more and more serious the further up the social scale the liege stood – the magnitude of the crime had far more to do with the status of the person offended against than any absolute justice. Indeed, Saxon and Celtic law codes of this time specified penalties that had to be paid for different offences depending on the status of the victim. This was most common in the case of murder or injury, where the fine for killing a rich noble might be twenty times the fine for killing a landless peasant, but there are also codes where it costs more if you start a brawl in front of an archbishop than in front of a mere bishop!

Anselm pictures God as the ultimate liege-lord, infinite in honour and majesty, and so deserving of infinite obedience; and thinking like this, Boso is then forced to confess that it would be better for whole worlds to be destroyed than for someone to glance out the window, if the glance was an act of disobedience to God.

If, then, the slightest sin is a crime of unimaginable, infinite, seriousness because it is a crime against God, who is infinitely majestic, what can be done about it?

Let's go back to the law codes: if someone committed murder, the punishment was (almost always) death; however, instead of being executed, they could pay a fine ('satisfaction') to the family of the victim, the amount of the fine again being dependent on the social status of the person they murdered. Anselm suggests that we might imagine God's reaction to sin working in the same way: either it must be punished, which means eternal torment in hell, or an equivalent satisfaction must be offered to God. At this point Anselm says something very interesting: God created human beings to worship and serve him, so it is inconceivable that God would simply punish sin – that would mean that his plans for creation had been frustrated. So instead some appropriate satisfaction must be offered. The satisfaction must be offered by a human being, but the amount demanded is infinite, and only God can possibly offer an infinite payment, so God must become incarnate – be born as a human being – for this to work.

The answer, then, is Jesus. But, like every human being, Jesus owes God a life of complete obedience and utter worship, so all the things he does with his life, praiseworthy and wonderful though they are, are no more than God already deserves, and so cannot be any part of the satisfaction. However, having lived a sinless life, Jesus is not subject to the curse which says all sinners will die, so by offering his life he can give to God something that God could not demand, and so make satisfaction for the sins of the whole world. As someone has described it, the cross is 'a gift exceeding every debt', and that is why it saves us.

Anselm's ideas were very influential and very controversial then, and continue to be so.

Abelard

Anselm was opposed almost immediately by another writer, Peter Abelard (who is remembered these days mostly for his tragic love affair with Heloise). Abelard did not write a book on the atonement as Anselm did, but in a brief note in a commentary on Romans he suggests that God does not need any sacrifice or satisfaction or ransom to forgive us – he can do it just because he loves us. Why, then, did Jesus die on the cross? Abelard suggests that it was a demonstration of God's love, the ultimate act of self-sacrifice which teaches us just how much God loves us and inspires us to love God in gratitude in return, and to love other human beings like Jesus loved us.

As medieval theology developed, most writers wanted to agree with both Anselm and Abelard: the idea that Jesus' death was a satisfaction for our sin became very influential (probably because it picked up all the biblical language of sacrifice and ransom without any of the problems of earlier ideas); at the same time, the idea that we should be inspired by the love of Jesus to love similarly was also very attractive. Alongside this, many people believed that we could be healed through eating and drinking the body and blood of Jesus, and so stressed the role of the sacrament in salvation.

Thomas Aquinas

St Thomas Aquinas, widely regarded as the greatest mind in the medieval church, lived about 150 years after Anselm. He offered several accounts of how Christ's suffering brought salvation, picking up various terms from the Scriptures and from earlier theologians.

He first of all agreed with Anselm that the death of Christ was a satisfaction for sin. Defining satisfaction as something offered that outweighs the earlier offence, he said that since the gift of Christ's life on the cross overwhelmingly outweighed every sin because of the infinite value of the divine Son's own life, the Father, having received this gift, put aside all thoughts of human sin.

Thomas next asked about sacrifice, which he understood as a gift offered to God with a good heart, which Christ's self-offering was.

Finally he looked at redemption, which he divided into two parts: redemption from slavery to the devil (so the cross as ransom), and redemption from the punishment due to sin. He affirmed that the death of Jesus redeems us in both these ways: we are ransomed from slavery and freed from our punishment.

Although in his list of the effects of Christ's suffering Thomas did not talk about the inspiring nature of Jesus' life and death, he did speak elsewhere of the way Jesus on the cross models for us the virtues of obedience, humility, forbearance and so on. Thus he included Peter Abelard's ideas in his wider theology as well.

John Duns Scotus

Abelard's theology was taken up more broadly by John Duns Scotus, who lived in the generation after Thomas and opposed him on several issues (not least for political reasons: Thomas was a Dominican and Scotus a Franciscan, and the two orders were bitter rivals).

Scotus held that as Christ suffered as a human being, the worth of his suffering was not infinite (as demanded by Anselm and assumed by Thomas), but limited. How, then, could Christ's sufferings save us? Scotus argued, essentially, that there was no actual need for any satisfaction, sacrifice, payment, or anything else, but that God could choose to do what he would and to accept as adequate whatever he liked. (This idea of the unlimited freedom of God is a big part of Scotus's theology.) So, as Peter Abelard had argued, there was no need for Christ to die for our forgiveness, but God chose to save us through the sufferings of Christ.

Typology and Symbolism

One final theme in Thomas is worth noting: he gathers up and presents many fruits of the ancient and medieval tradition of interpreting the cross typologically and symbolically. There are long lists of types drawn from the Old Testament that the cross fulfils, thus making the cross an appropriate way for Christ to have died. The fact that Adam's first sin involved a tree makes Christ's dying on a tree particularly appropriate. And the cross is made of wood, just like the ark in which Noah and all creation was saved, the altar on which the sacrifices were offered, and so on.

We might find this sort of identification slightly fanciful, but medieval readers of the Bible believed passionately that every text spoke of Jesus Christ somehow, and so they enjoyed and appreciated this.

The symbolic interpretations consist in looking at the cross itself and finding appropriate symbols there. So Thomas records one author saying that a cross pointing in four directions indicates that the salvation of Christ is for everyone everywhere. Another suggests that by being lifted up from the earth on a hill, Jesus reveals that his death will take us to heaven.

Again, I suppose that most of us today will find these arguments strange or difficult, but they were an important part of how our Christian sisters and brothers of old understood the cross.

Where does all this Leave Penal Substitution?

As Christians we have always known that we are saved by Jesus. In the early centuries of the church this fact was simply assumed and argued from, and not only in relation to Jesus' death – the incarnation was somehow involved as well. Writers talked about Jesus' death in terms of ransom and sacrifice and healing and victory without giving fully worked out theories of exactly how these things were accomplished by his death; and they often saw his incarnation as healing human nature in some mysterious way, without working that out fully either.

Some people tried to come up with more careful explanations of how this all happened, but these tended to be very obviously unsatisfactory in one way or another. Anselm offered perhaps the first really convincing worked through account of how we are saved by Jesus, seeing the death of Jesus as a satisfaction paid to God so that the sins of humanity will be overlooked rather than punished. By the time we get to Thomas Aquinas, this had become one picture to put alongside several others in offering a presentation of how Christ's death saves us. Peter Abelard and John Duns Scotus developed an alternative view, based on the idea that there was no particular need for Christ to have died for us to be saved.

In all this discussion and development there has been almost nothing that looks like penal substitution as evangelicals have understood it.

I want to make three comments about that.

First, people sometimes claim to find penal substitutionary atonement in the church fathers in particular. As I have indicated, I can find one isolated passage in Gregory the Great, but nothing else. When I look at the texts where people claim to find the fathers talking in penal substitutionary terms, I almost always find language of ransom or sacrifice. This seems to be read by some modern readers as if it should be understood as penal substitution.

Second, recent critics of penal substitution have often accused Anselm of starting the tradition. This is just wrong: Anselm did *not* believe that Christ was punished in our place; rather he believed that Christ offered his life to the Father so that there was no longer any need for punishment. Both pro-penal substitution writers reading the fathers and anti-penal substitution writers reading Anselm make the same mistake of finding a penal account when actually a quite different picture was intended by the writers concerned. There is a good reason why people have been so prone to this mistake, which I will come to in chapter six.

Third, what should we make of the lack of teaching of penal substitution in the first fifteen hundred years of church history? I think it is going to depend on how we expect the doctrine of atonement to work out. If we think there should be only one right way of understanding the atonement that is there in all the

Scriptures and held on to by at least the majority of church teachers, we are going to be embarrassed – but not just by penal substitution – there is no other account either of the atonement that
even begins to meet these criteria. If we understand the various
pictures of the atonement to be complementary and (only) partial
attempts to grab hold of a bigger truth, as I am suggesting we do,
then the history of the early and medieval church will not seem
surprising to us.

The Reformers are the thinkers who finally bring penal substitution to the centre stage, and the next chapter begins with them.

Five

'See all Your Sins On Jesus Laid!'

The Cross in Christian History (2)

See all your sins on Jesus laid:
The Lamb of God was slain,
His soul was once an offering made
For every soul of man.

(Charles Wesley, 'O for a Thousand Tongues')

Where did the Story of Penal Substitution Come From?

There was a way of teaching church history, common in Britain a generation ago, that dealt with the first centuries of the church and then ignored about a thousand years to pick up the story again at the Reformation.

While we have to be selective in what we teach, as there is just not time to cover everything, and while the choices made then may have been the right ones, somehow, though, one could come away with the wrong impression: that the history and progress of the church ground to a halt on November 1, 451 AD (the last day of the Council of Chalcedon) and only began again on October 31, 1517, the day on which popular memory has Martin Luther nailing ninety-five theses to the door of All Saints Church in Wittenberg. (He actually probably just wrote a letter, but it's a good story!)

One of the problems with thinking like this is the idea that the Reformation appeared out of nowhere – an astonishing transformation. Actually, most of the classic Reformation ideas are around, and being debated, in the years before Luther's birth; at the Reformation the arguments become part of the reason for the church splitting. (There are various other reasons, notably political ones, for example Henry VIII's break from Rome and the founding of the Church of England.)

Martin Luther's complaint, whether nailed to a door or mailed in a letter, was about the sale of 'indulgences'.

What are indulgences?

Catholic doctrine taught that any sin committed brought both guilt and penalty on the sinner, and that that guilt could be forgiven through sacramental confession and the penalty paid off through penance. Any 'unpaid' penalty at death would be worked off through time in purgatory before the soul could enjoy heaven. An indulgence is a promise issued by the pope or another bishop that essentially 'paid off' a certain amount of due penalty for the recipient.

Luther complained about the way these were being sold to raise money to build St Peter's Church in Rome. Luther was, at the time, struggling with his own conscience, very aware of his own sinfulness, and not able to trust the assurances that the sacraments and penance could help him. In the course of all this, his lecturing on the Scriptures led him to the startling realisation that Christ by his death had done all that was necessary for him to be accepted and forgiven by God. All he had to do was believe in the free forgiveness and righteousness God offered. This was the great Reformation claim of 'salvation by faith alone'.

All the Reformers were (rightly!) anxious to hold on to the idea that salvation is a free gift of God in Christ, not something we earn for ourselves. Because of this, they made a particularly sharp distinction between 'justification' (being declared innocent and righteous and acceptable before God) and 'sanctification' (the process of gradually growing in holiness and Christ-likeness). These two things had not been distinguished so clearly before (indeed, the official Roman Catholic response to the Reformation, the Council of Trent, refused to make the distinction).

When we try to think about the cross with this distinction in mind, and then try to describe what Jesus did for us on the cross, we are likely to end up preferring explanations that emphasise an external change of status rather than an internal change of nature.

That is, if you think like this, it is much easier to think of the atonement in terms of forgiveness or cleansing than healing or transformation.

In fact, due to some themes in the culture of their day, almost all the Reformers ended up thinking about the cross in legal terms: we were guilty, and the work of Jesus somehow made us innocent – more, it made us honoured citizens.

This is not very far from Anselm's ideas, of course, but the changing culture meant the Reformers told a different story of salvation to the one Anselm had told. His story involved a personal offence against a majestic superior, God; the Reformers told the story more in terms of an offence against an implacable law.

The reasons for this are fairly easy to discern: in 1215, a century or so after Anselm died, the then Archbishop of Canterbury was meeting with King John and his nobles at Runnymede, just south of what is now Heathrow Airport. John was made to sign a document there, the 'Great Charter' or Magna Carta, that granted various rights and corrected certain abuses. The reason Magna Carta is celebrated and remembered still today, however, is because of an idea that underlies it: the idea that there are some things that even kings can't do; that there is a law of justice in the universe that is unbreakable and cannot be set aside. By the time of the Reformers, this idea had become normal. So, instead of Anselm's story about an angry monarch, they told a story about the unbreakable demands of justice – a story that we now call 'penal substitution'.

Martin Luther

The Reformers believed that wrongdoing demanded punishment; Anselm's old idea that a gift given to the offended party as 'satisfaction' might remove the need for punishment was gone – that would be like trying to bribe a judge! If sin had been committed, punishment must follow – that was simple justice. If God was going to act to save us from that punishment, it was not by somehow ignoring or perverting justice, but by finding a way of meeting the demands of justice that meant we did not have to endure them.

Martin Luther began to understand that way as an act of substitution. Commenting on Galatians 3:13 ('Christ redeemed us from the curse of the law, having become a curse for us . . .'), he pictures the Father sending the Son:

> He sent his Son into the world, heaped all the sins of all upon him, and said to him, 'You, be Peter the denier; Paul the persecutor, blasphemer, and assaulter; David the adulterer; the sinner who ate the apple in Paradise; the thief on the cross. In short, you be the person of all people, the one who has committed the sins of all people . . .' Now the Law comes and says, 'I find that sinner taking on himself the sin of all people; I see no other sins but those in him. So let him die on the cross!' And so it attacks him and kills him. This done, the whole world is purged of all sin . . . (My translation)

Luther doesn't pause to explain how the transformation came about – that would be for others to work out later. What is interesting, though, is the role of the law here. It 'comes' and speaks and acts. And it is the law, rather than the devil, or God, or corruption, or anything else, that we need saving from. Luther always had a very negative view of the law, but this is what began to set the tone for how other Reformers understood the cross. Luther is also, here, talking in plainly substitutionary terms: Christ dies instead of us.

John Calvin

The first full statement of penal substitution that I know comes in the writings of John Calvin.

Calvin spent most of his life as a pastor to the church in Geneva and devoted himself to taking the church, and students preparing for the ministry, through the Scriptures. He wrote his *Institutes of the Christian Religion* as an introduction to the concepts and arguments that people needed to understand to help them read Scripture for themselves. When he turns to explaining the work of Christ there, he begins like this: 'Since God is a righteous Judge, he does not allow his law to be broken without punishment, but is equipped to avenge it' (*Institutes* II.xvi.1).

And with that we are immediately in the thought world of law and punishment.

Calvin would use many different images to describe the way Christ's work saves us (he talks about victory and healing, amongst others), but the focus is on a worked-out account of penal substitution.

The story begins with the love of God: God acted to save us because of his love, mercy and grace towards us. But God is a righteous judge, committed to his own law. He cannot ignore it, or be bought off; it must be upheld. And we come before him as guilty sinners, deserving of punishment. So God comes himself, in the person of his Son, and takes our guilt on himself. On the cross, Christ bears the punishment of all that guilt, and so justice is satisfied and God can welcome us as he always desired to.

Calvin does not, like Luther, view the law as an enemy: for him the law is good and right, which is why God must uphold it. Nor does Calvin see quite such a literal transfer of sin as Luther did. Christ does not *become* Peter the denier; rather, the *guilt* of Peter's betrayal is *transferred* to Christ, and so the punishment is born by Christ.

Can guilt actually be transferred like this?

Calvin justifies the idea of such a transfer in two ways – neither of them entirely satisfactory. One goes roughly: 'Scripture says it happens, particularly in the sacrifices, so obviously it can happen.' The other stresses Paul's language of Christians being united with Christ, or 'in Christ', and so says the transfer is between two people who are already connected in some important way by God.

This question will remain for the later tradition, but in Calvin, at last, we find full-blown penal substitution.

Anabaptists and Anglicans

Of course, not all those who left the Roman Catholic church in the sixteenth century agreed with Luther or Calvin.

The Anabaptist movement, for example, tended to emphasise a process of suffering with Christ over any account of salvation through Christ's sufferings. It was also very suspicious of the Lutheran and Reformed separation of justification from sanctification, which looked like an invitation to claim Christian faith without any need to live the life of a disciple.

The Anglican *Book of Homilies*, like the *Book of Common Prayer*, tends to mix language of justice and ransom together in a way that is distinctive, if slightly confusing.

Other isolated individuals rejected the need for any redemption at all.

But Calvin's description of penal substitution seemed to be the most powerful story of salvation on offer. It became the official teaching of most of the Reformed and Lutheran churches, and the common understanding of most Reformed, Lutheran and Anglican writers for the next two centuries.

The Evangelical Revival and After

When the Evangelical Revival began with Wesley, Whitefield and Edwards in the 1730s, penal substitutionary explanations of the atonement were common. This was not the only way of speaking of the cross, but it was certainly the most important and significant.

It is therefore no surprise to find almost all the early evangelical leaders talking about the cross in penal terms. However, all of them would cheerfully use other language as well, and many of them would use other images far more often than penal ones. Some emphasised penal substitution more than others; it is noticeable, for instance, that John Wesley's sermons and tracts interpret the cross in penal terms far more often than do Charles Wesley's hymns.

Penal substitution at this point in history was just a normal way of talking about the atonement in the Church of England; it was not something new, dreamt up by the evangelicals, or something held to only by a strange bunch of fanatics. John Wesley, for example, used penal substitutionary language in his tract *The Character of a Methodist*, which was written to defend the orthodoxy (and, incidentally, sanity!) of himself and his followers. He described what he believed about the atonement in straightforwardly penal terms, assuming everyone would recognise this as standard Anglican orthodoxy.

(Incidentally, in the eighteenth century the word enthusiast carried the same sense as *fanatic* does today, and the evangelicals were often accused of being 'enthusiasts'. I have heard that there is a monument in a parish church in Cambridge somewhere commemorating a vicar who served for many years 'without ever once showing any trace of enthusiasm'. I've never found it, but I really hope it's true!)

However, as I've said, common as penal substitution was at the time, the evangelicals were prepared also to use other pictures, other stories, to describe the wonderful salvation won by Jesus on the cross. In *Hymns for the Use of People Called Methodists* (written mostly by Charles Wesley, but edited for orthodoxy by John before publication), language of sacrifice is far more common than language of penal substitution (perhaps because Charles was often quoting biblical language directly). Indeed, one hymn uses at least twelve different images for the atonement (including healing, restoration, a change of clothes, the gift of riches), but does not even touch penal imagery. A few pages later, though, Charles would write:

> Guilty I stand before thy face
> On me I feel thy wrath abide
> 'Tis just the sentence should take place
> 'Tis just – but Oh! thy Son hath died!

*   *   *

> For me I now believe he died
> He made my every crime his own
> Fully for me he satisfied
> Father, well-pleased behold thy Son!

This is about as straightforward an account of penal substitution as occurs in any hymn anywhere, so Charles was certainly not opposed to the idea, but he seemed to prefer to tell the story of salvation in other ways.

Jonathan Edwards was a pastor in the American colonies, and the best mind amongst the early evangelicals. Again, he is comfortable and happy to use the language of penal substitution, but appears in his writings about the cross to be restlessly casting about for new ways to speak of it. He develops new stories of salvation, probably because he wants new, different, and striking images for a people who have heard the gospel over and over and become hardened to gospel preaching.

If we went through the other leaders, we would find the same story: penal substitution is there, but it is not the only thing. It took its place alongside quotations of the biblical language of sacrifice and redemption, and many other pictures, as a way of describing what Christ had done on the cross.

Criticism of Penal Substitution

The first evangelical I could find who criticised penal substitution was a Baptist pastor and theologian, Andrew Fuller, writing about 1800. I don't think Fuller realised he was changing the doctrine, but he believed that guilt cannot be transferred from one person to another – and if you believe this, then you cannot talk about Jesus taking our guilt and suffering for us.

This question – of whether guilt can be transferred – was later addressed by Charles Hodge, the great Princeton theologian from the middle of the nineteenth century.

Hodge distinguished between two senses of the word *guilt*, saying it means both the psychological consciousness of having done wrong, and the legal liability to punishment. He argued that while of course guilt in the first sense could not be transferred, there was no reason at all that guilt in the second sense could not be, and on this basis the atonement could still be understood as penal substitution.

I will say more about this argument in the next chapter.

Other evangelicals in the early nineteenth century began to question penal substitution as well. A group of brilliant young Scots thinkers – John McLeod Campbell, Thomas Erskine of Linlathlen, and Edward Irving chief among them – led the questioning. McLeod Campbell's great argument was essentially against the idea that wrongdoing demands punishment. He felt that the implacable law, which Calvin had imagined, was morally repulsive. Erskine thought the same thing, but also questioned the effects of the atonement if understood in a penal way: the mere forgiveness of guilt is not enough; the atonement must lead to some form of moral transformation in our lives as well.

These questions were not new. The earliest hints of a position like this go all the way back to the sixteenth century, to an uncle and nephew named Laelius and Faustus Socinus, the latter being the founder of Unitarianism. Faustus Socinus wrote a powerful critique of the developing penal theory of the atonement which anticipated almost every argument used since, and has perhaps never been bettered. He believed that Jesus was not really divine, but just an inspired human being, and that his death was just an inspiring example of self-sacrifice. There was no need for any payment, punishment, or offering for God to forgive us; he did so out of love and mercy, and Jesus showed us how we should live selflessly and heroically in the light of God's free forgiveness.

Fuller, Erskine, and the rest didn't believe this. They believed the cross was vital, and an intrinsic part of how God saves us. They just didn't understand that salvation in penal terms.

The liberal theologians

In the nineteenth century, however, a growing number of theologians did agree with Socinus, thinking that there was no need for any payment, sacrifice, or punishment for us to be saved, and that Jesus' death was just an inspiring and noble demonstration of putting others before yourself. This was the developing 'liberal' movement in theology.

The characteristic liberal understanding of the atonement was reflected in the 'moral influence' theory: Jesus did not die to pay a price, but to witness to an ideal. His death affects us by inspiring us to give our lives to the same ideal. 'Love so amazing, so divine, demands my soul, my life, my all.'

Of course, it does indeed. I would hope that no evangelical would ever deny the enormous moral influence of the cross or the inspiring and powerful ways in which this idea was expressed by the greatest of the liberal theologians.

The question is whether there is more to be said than that.

The liberal theologians had two major complaints against penal substitution. First, they said, it was inappropriately supernaturalist: the idea that Jesus' death might somehow transform my life now, other than by being an inspiring story, smacked of the miraculous and magical, which the liberal tradition was uncomfortable with. (This, of course, was a criticism of almost any traditional theology of the atonement.) The second criticism was directed particularly at the once dominant penal theory and concerned the nature of justice. It was, liberals believed, simply barbaric to assume that God demanded a price of blood before he was prepared to forgive. To try to dress this up as justice, or the demands of some law of God, only compounded the offence.

As the nineteenth century came to a close, this was the settled position of most theologians. There were still conservative voices (and not just evangelicals) who argued for some account of payment, sacrifice, or punishment in their understanding of the cross, but they were decidedly a minority. (A historian of doctrine, L.W. Grensted, writing in 1919, claims to identify the last supporter of the penal theory in Germany, one Philippi, who died in 1882!)

On both sides, however, there was a broad assumption that different theories of atonement were in competition. Charles Hodge, for example, talked of 'the orthodox doctrine . . . common to the Latin, Lutheran and Reformed churches', and assumed he was giving an exposition of it, and that opposing views were defective if they did not agree with him. On the other side, R.C. Moberly's great *Atonement and Personality*, published in 1900, assumed the truth of a particular theory of moral influence, and explored (apparently sympathetically) the 'defects' and 'inadequacies' of all other views.

The Twentieth Century

Two interesting changes happened to this picture in the first half of the twentieth century.

Neo-orthodoxy

The first was the revival of more 'conservative' theories of atonement, and even of penal substitution, amongst serious theologians. The liberal theology of the nineteenth century had assumed people were basically decent, good, and civilised and developed a theory of atonement to fit this picture. As we've seen, they said all that was needed for us to be changed and made holy was an inspiring example of the way we could and should live; having once seen Jesus, we would want to be like him, and that desire, coupled with our own energies, was enough.

Perhaps Anselm's great complaint, 'You have not yet considered how serious a thing sin is!', should have been heard with more force, but nineteenth-century Europe was optimistic and believed in the inevitable progress of all cultures to a peak of civilisation which (it thought) it was on the cusp of reaching.

The battle of the Somme put an end to all that.

Actually, the cultural mood had begun changing before the war. For example, G.K. Chesterton, recalling that period in the dedicatory poem to *The Man who was Thursday*, writes: 'Science announced non-entity, and Art admired decay. The world was old, and ended . . .).

But the decadence or despair of 'advanced' artists and poets could largely be ignored. The carnage on the fields of Flanders could not – at least not in Europe.

I was talking yesterday to some of my American students, who were astonished at the sheer number of war memorials in Britain. I pointed out to them that every village had lost several – sometimes several dozen – of its young men; that's why there is a memorial in every village. What now of the belief that evil was merely the result of primitive culture, and Europe's glittering civilisation had almost done away with it?

In theology the new mood became known as 'neo-orthodoxy'. Led by Karl Barth in Europe and Richard and Reinhold Niebuhr in America, theologians looked again at the degradation and desperate need of man, and at the amazing promise of the gospel that an almighty God had acted in astonishing and decisive ways to change that.

Supernaturalism was back on the agenda: only something unknown, unheard, marvellous, a decisive break-in of a wholly different world, could help or save us. Sin and evil were real and serious and powerful; education would not save us, and nor would our own desire to civilise. We stand in need of re-creation by an external power.

Emil Brunner, an early friend of Karl Barth's and a leader of the movement in his own right, explored this in explicitly penal terms and rewrote the old doctrine of penal substitution for a new generation of theologians. Since Brunner's time a resurgence of evangelical theology has led to a number of serious and sympathetic discussions of penal substitution from within the evangelical tradition.

Gustav Aulén

The second shift in the early part of the twentieth century also involved a renewed awareness of the reality of evil.

Gustav Aulén, a Swedish theologian, published a book in 1930 called *Christus Victor: An historical study of the three main types of the idea of the Atonement.* In it he acknowledged that the argument of the day was between a group of conservative views stressing the cross as the paying of a price somehow, and a group of liberal views stressing the cross as an inspiring example. He wanted to claim that both were wrong, and that the proper way to understand the cross was what he called the 'classic' view (which has since become known as the 'Christus victor' view, in honour of Aulén's book). Aulén thought that the New Testament, and the early church fathers, were best understood as picturing the cross as a battle between Jesus and the powers of evil, and the resurrection as Jesus' decisive victory.

Aulén was trying to add a third possible position to the two already available, but in retrospect his book was more important for other reasons. His biblical and historical work had the same problem as earlier attempts to find a united theory of the atonement: he ended up forcing all the different pictures to fit his favoured understanding. But he did begin to widen the range of ways in which people thought they might understand the atonement.

Aulén was not claiming to have discovered how the atonement worked, but rather that he had a good story to tell about it, a story that could not be broken down into careful logical arguments. He described his view as 'dramatic' rather than logical.

In the 1960s, Aulén's attempt to expand the number of possible theories of atonement, and his idea that what we needed to do was tell dramatic stories about it, came together. A series of books on the atonement appeared which did not try to say one theory was right and another wrong, but that each of the theories pointed in a helpful, though partial, way to the one awesome truth of the atonement. Generally, writers stopped talking about 'theories' of the atonement and used more modest terms: F.W. Dillistone wrote of 'analogues' and 'parables'; John McIntyre of 'models'; and Colin Gunton of 'metaphors'. I am following these writers in this book and using the different terms (and my own 'stories of salvation') fairly interchangeably.

The latter half of the twentieth century

Dillistone, McIntyre and their contemporaries bring us right to the end of the twentieth century.

At the same time as they were working, another significant move was taking place, beginning in Medellín in Columbia in 1968. There, a conference of Latin American Roman Catholic bishops met to consider the invitation of the recent Second Vatican Council to make the (Roman Catholic) church more relevant locally. They responded in an unexpected direction, combining traditional theological themes with a powerful awareness of the pressing poverty of many of their people, and the causes of this in the social, political and economic forces that caused that poverty.

And so through the 1970s, a 'theology of liberation' developed which tried to make theology relevant to the poorest people in the world.

Liberation theology has been controversial (particularly because of its relation to Marxist thought), but it has led to two big changes in the way theology has been done in the last generation or two. First, theologians have learned to ask about the ethical implications of an idea, including the unintended ones. Second, 'contextual theologies' (theologies done consciously from this or that context) have become important and common. The most significant in the Western world has been feminist theology, and there have been others, including urban theology and black theology.

A doctrine of atonement, then, is now no longer just about salvation at the end of time; it is now seen as having to address questions like the following: Does it serve to liberate people (poor people, women, ethnic minorities, or whoever) here and now, or does it encourage their oppression? Does it still appear to liberate if looked at from the particular standpoint of this or that oppressed group?

It may be that this is not how theology should be done, and scholars are also arguing about that.

The questions are surely good ones, however. As a preacher I would not want to stand in the pulpit week after week saying things that led to my people being unconcerned about poverty, or that gave comfort to racists. If someone claims that this or that idea does, then we need to think hard about whether the claim is true; if it is, perhaps we need to preach differently.

The doctrine of atonement, and penal substitution in particular, has been accused of failures in these areas. A general complaint has been the lack of any moral, and particularly social, impetus in the more conservative versions of the doctrine. It is all very well claiming that Jesus has paid the price for my sin, but in what way does that change the way I live in the world? Sin is not just an individual reality; it is also something communal and structural that leads to the oppression of the poor, the exploitation of children, and the dehumanisation of women; how, then, does a doctrine of atonement address these realities?

The particular questions addressed to penal substitution have been concerned with, and reflected concern about, its apparent celebration of violence, seen particularly in the powerful picture of Jesus as the uncomplaining victim of violence. Feminist theologians in particular have asked what this doctrine says to those who perpetrate domestic abuse, and to those who suffer abuse. If Jesus 'was silent like a sheep before its shearers' (Is. 53:7) because 'it was the Lord's will to crush him with pain' (Is. 53:10), should a woman who is regularly beaten by her partner remain silent, accepting her own suffering as the Lord's will? Most recently, some feminist theologians have seized on the particular Father-Son violence of penal substitution and said that it is little more than an account of 'divine child abuse'.

These accusations are serious, and need to be taken seriously. I will return to them in chapter eight.

Summary: The Atonement and Penal Substitution in Christian History

Christian theologians and preachers have told many, many 'stories of salvation'. They have drawn pictures of kings being ransomed and slaves being freed and the sick being healed and guilty prisoners being declared innocent, of human nature being transformed and evil powers being defeated and people being inspired to a new life. The stories have changed through time because culture has changed through time, and different stories communicate the unchanging reality of the gospel to different cultures. At the time of the Reformation, penal substitution became a common and successful way of talking about the cross. Despite some critics, this remained the case for several centuries.

Over the past two hundred years, however, several significant criticisms have been raised. Any account of penal substitution today needs to answer three questions:

1. How are all the different 'stories of salvation' related?
2. How did penal substitution ever thrive as an idea in early modern culture (i.e. sixteenth to eighteenth centuries)?
3. What, if anything, has changed?

Can the hard questions that have been put, be answered?

Chapter six will address the first of these, chapter seven the second, and chapter eight the last.

Six

'Who Can Ever Say They Understand?'

Pictures of the Cross

Who can ever say they understand
All the wonders of his masterplan?
Christ came down and gave himself for man
For evermore . . .
(Dave Bilbrough, 'Who can ever say . . .' © 1989 Thankyou Music)

Which is Right and Which is Wrong?

Healing, sacrifice, ransom, satisfaction, example, penal substitution – and dozens of others . . . In the Bible, and through Christian history, the profoundest thinkers, the most powerful preachers, the most inspiring worship leaders, and the most devout pray-ers have reached for many, many different pictures to try to understand what Jesus did for us on the cross, to grasp 'the wonders of his master plan'. We know he saved us, cancelled our sin, set us free, gave us his Holy Spirit, allowed us to come to his Father in prayer and worship, opened up the promise of eternal life. We know all the wonderful gifts of our salvation. The question, however, is always *how* Christ's death wins these gifts for us. And all the different pictures of the cross are just different ways to try to explain that. Christians tell, and always have told, all sorts of different 'stories of salvation', how Jesus' life and death and resurrection heals us, or inspires us, or pays the price for our sins. In this chapter I want to ask what we do with all these different pictures or stories – how do we decide between them, which is right and which is wrong?

Indeed, *do* we *have* to decide between them?

We might want to say one picture, one story, is right, and all the others are wrong. Evangelicals have often wanted to say that the proper way of understanding what Jesus did on the cross is to think of it in terms of penal substitution: our sins deserved to be punished; Jesus took the punishment in our place; so now we are set free from our sins. That is the truth of the matter. All the other pictures and stories are either ways of illustrating this central truth, or just wrong.

As we have just seen, however, in the nineteenth century liberal Christians often felt the same way about the 'moral example' picture: on the cross, Jesus demonstrated the ultimate self-sacrifice, inspiring all those of us who see it, to love like he did and to follow his example.

Gustav Aulén thought both of these were wrong, and that the true picture was of Jesus winning the victory over the powers of sin and death and hell.

In recent debates amongst British evangelicals about penal substitution, this approach (of there being only one right 'story') has been assumed. One account of the cross must be right, the others either wrong or incomplete. On one side, the assumption has been that penal substitution is what must be asserted: anything else is a mere illustration of – or indeed a distraction from – this one fundamental truth. On the other side, a standard has recently been raised with Aulén for the 'Christus victor' idea: this is the true doctrine, and other things are distortions or half-truths. On both sides, however, the assumption that the only way to do atonement theology is to look for the one right answer has reigned unquestioned.

There are several problems with thinking like this. The most obvious is that, as I've tried to show, the Bible itself doesn't have just one picture for how Jesus saves us. Indeed, even some single sentences in the Bible don't have just one picture for how Jesus saves us! In chapter one I pointed to three completely different pictures in Romans 3:24–25 alone; to that we could add Ephesians 1:5–7 (two sentences in most translations, but one in the Greek), which speaks of adoption, 'redemption through his blood' and forgiveness, in rapid succession.

Even in the classic passage from Isaiah 53 there are two very different pictures side by side: the bit all our songs quote is in verse 5: 'he was wounded for our transgressions, crushed for our iniquities, the punishment that made us whole was upon him.' Here there is no question that the story is of sin and its punishment being inflicted on another, Jesus, so that we can be set free from the consequences of our wrongdoing. In verse 4, however, we read that the Servant, Jesus, 'has borne our infirmities and carried our diseases', and the picture is a strange medical one of Jesus drawing the infection or the poison out of us, and so healing us by taking our diseases on himself.

(There is a very modern example of this latter kind of thinking at the end of the first series of the new *Doctor Who* – a British science fiction television programme that has become an institution – where Billie Piper's character, Rose, absorbs the Tardis's 'time vortex' into herself, and the Doctor, knowing she will not be able to bear it, draws it out of her into his own body. This destroys him, but he is able to regenerate. There are worse illustrations of what Isaiah was talking about!)

In chapters two and three I tried to give a list of some of the ways in which the Bible talks about Jesus saving us. I came up with eight in the New Testament alone, and it would not be difficult to add more if we wanted to.

Now of course we could say that all these different biblical pictures are actually just different illustrations of the one 'true' truth. But it doesn't look much like that to me. There doesn't seem to be that much careful organisation of the different pictures, or any hint that this one or that one is just an illustration of the other. Look back at the passages I have quoted from Romans and Ephesians and Isaiah: these don't look like accounts where one picture is central and the others just illustrate it – the pictures are put right next to one another with no suggestion that one is more important than the other. If the Bible had wanted to teach us that there was just one way of understanding the cross, then it could have made it a whole lot clearer!

This strange aspect of the Bible's witness to the cross was less of a problem for the liberal theologians in the nineteenth century, because they could just claim that the Bible represented the 'primitive' and 'barbaric' worldview of its times. That meant that all those rather uncivilised pictures of sacrifice and judicial executions and so on needed to be removed to find the essential spiritual truth of the matter.

There is a grain of truth in this view that we need to take seriously. The Bible is a human book as well as a divine one, and in inspiring the biblical authors, the Holy Spirit did not bypass or remove their humanity. Because of this we should expect to find differences of interest and emphasis in the different books. For example, the author of Hebrews is far more interested in the Old Testament background of priests and temple sacrifices than Paul, who is always writing to Gentile churches. But even so, the Bible just doesn't look as though it is trying to give us one central truth of how Jesus saves us, with lots of supporting illustrations – that's just not the way it's written.

There is, however, another reason for supposing that we should not assume that only one of the stories of salvation is a true account of what went on at the cross: all of these stories work by assuming a particular background. Sacrifice makes sense only within the context of a certain religious system and a temple; redemption pictures the slave market, with a price needing to be paid for a slave to go free; penal substitution invokes the image of a law court, with a legal penalty imposed that must be endured somehow. Indeed, in chapters four and five we saw some pictures that were once very important in Christian history, but are no longer used at all. In each case they were forgotten because they assumed a world of thought that is now just alien – 'physicalism', assuming something about the reality of 'human nature'; Anselm's satisfaction theory, assuming a feudal society – and so they don't make any sense to us anymore.

So every story of salvation works by picturing what Christ did on the cross in terms of one particular facet of human experience, whether it be religious (sacrifice), legal (penal), or whatever. If we want to say that one or another of these theories is just plain right, then we have to say that the atonement, what Christ did for us to save us, really is just one example of the some more general part of human life. There are lots of sacrifices in the world, and the death of Jesus is one more. Perhaps more powerful, more lasting, than any of the others, but still, just a sacrifice amongst sacrifices. Or Jesus is one amongst a number of inspiring moral examples that we may find. Again, perhaps the most inspiring, but still, an example of some more general aspect of human life.

But this presents a problem: the cross of Christ is far too fundamental, far too basic, to be just one example of some more general part of human life. When the Bible talks about 'the Lamb slain before the foundation of the world' (Rev. 13:8), there is a hint of this. Perhaps it is clearer in a text like 1 John 4:9–10: 'This is love: not that we loved God, but that God loved us, and gave his Son as an atoning sacrifice for our sins', where it seems that love is defined by what Jesus did for us on the cross, not the other way around. We do not understand the cross as just one example of love, or even as the supreme example as love – we understand love as one example of the cross.

Equally, Hebrews seems to suggest that the whole sacrificial system makes sense only when we read it in the light of Jesus' death, which might explain why the way sacrifice works is never spelled out in the Old Testament – they couldn't understand how sacrifice works, they didn't have a chance, until Jesus came and lived and died and rose again.

So we should not try to understand the cross of Christ through thinking about sacrifice, or love, or anything else in the world; rather, we should understand sacrifice, and love, and every other human reality by thinking about the cross of Christ. And if we take the view that only one of the stories of salvation is true, we end up denying this.

The Centrality of the Cross

What, then, is the alternative view?

Most theologians who have written about the cross of Jesus in the last few decades have, in one way or another, tried to say that we should hold on to all the stories of salvation. We should not pick one and discard, or downplay, the others.

This looks far more like the biblical practice, where, as we've seen, a lot of different pictures are piled up on top of one another with no real shape or order.

But how can we make sense of this?

If it is true that all these stories of salvation are really different, that a story about temples and priests and sacrifices is a completely different story from one about judges and law courts and punishments, then surely if one is right the other must be wrong?

But if the cross of Jesus really is as fundamental as I have described it, then we might say in response that we just *can't* give an accurate description of what happened when God saved us. Sacrifice and punishment and inspiring example and the rest of the stories of salvation we tell are like the parables that Jesus told. Jesus told us about God by telling stories of a farmer who had two sons, or a king who forgave his servant's debt, or a vineyard owner's dealings with his rebellious tenants. And each parable points to vital truth about who God is, but in a slightly oblique way. So why didn't Jesus just tell us 'God is loving and forgiving, but jealous and demanding too'?

I suspect the answer is that we wouldn't have understood well enough what even those apparently simple words meant. So instead, Jesus told us parables, drawing on common human experience which could be used to explain or illuminate the character of God.

And so it is with the stories of salvation we tell about the cross of Christ: each one gives us a glimpse of something so basic, so fundamental to human existence, and indeed to the whole of creation, that we don't have words to describe it – a glimpse of what God has done in Jesus.

Paul at the start begins the game: 'You know when you buy a slave's freedom? It's a bit like that! Or when the priest sacrifices the lamb in the temple – it's a bit like that too. Or when a country pays a ransom to gets its king back – a bit like that as well . . .' And the history I've described in the last two chapters is a history of people doing the same thing: grabbing hold of pictures, telling stories, that attempt to illuminate something of the wondrous cross.

I suspect most of them knew that the stories they were telling were not the whole truth. Calvin might have focused on penal substitution, but very consciously used six or seven other ways of talking about the cross also, so it is difficult to believe that he thought penal substitution was the only answer. Often enough people wrote because they thought the pictures other people were using were wrong, dishonouring to God and the gospel. Anselm felt that way about ransom, and Abelard in turn about

Anselm's own suggestions. But my sense is that it is only when we get into the nineteenth century that anyone really begins to believe that they have 'got it', that they are telling the truth, the whole truth and nothing but the truth about the cross. I think this was a mistake. We need many pictures, many stories, many facets of the one awesome truth of what Jesus has done.

I sometimes suggest to my students that they might find an illustration of this in the variety of different words used to describe the taste of a fine wine or – as we are in Scotland – whisky! The taster on television, or the tasting notes, will list a whole string of different words in an attempt to capture the one, indescribable, taste of the drink. The eighteen year old version of my favourite single malt whisky, Highland Park, for instance, is described by Michael Jackson (no, not that one . . .) as 'Lightly salty. Leafy (vine leaves?), pine nuts. Lots of flavour development: nuts, honey, cinnamon, dryish ginger.' Each word captures a taste experience most of us know (although . . . 'vine leaves' . . .?) in the hope that by imagining the combination we may begin to grasp the rich complexity of the taste of this fine whisky. By telling, and telling well, all the stories of salvation, we begin to get some sense of the astonishing thing that Jesus has done for us.

If this way of thinking is right, then it raises some more questions: How many stories or pictures are there? How do we tell if this or that picture is a good one? Is penal substitution a good story to tell? The rest of this chapter will deal with these questions.

Counting the Metaphors

There have been two broad approaches amongst writers who have advocated a 'many metaphors' approach. The first has been to talk about a few broad classes of metaphors; the second has been to try to be more exact, and separate out all the metaphors.

Gustav Aulén had argued there were three basic approaches to the problem, which he called 'objective', 'subjective' and 'classic'.

The 'objective' approach began (he thought) with Anselm and included Calvin and the evangelicals, and anyone else who saw the death of Christ as in any way paying a price or making satisfaction.

The 'subjective' approach could be traced back to Abelard, and reached ascendancy in nineteenth-century liberal theology. Here, the effect of the death of Christ was, simply, 'subjective': it inspired or amazed or attracted us when we saw it, and that was the essence of its power.

Finally, the 'classic' account, which was Aulén's own preferred option and which he traced back to the New Testament and the early church and claimed to find in Luther also. Here, the basic idea is of Christ's death as a conflict, and the resurrection as a victory.

Other writers have taken up this threefold division, without the conflict between them, and argued that each is a helpful perspective on the question. This would be the broadest approach to the question.

Narrower approaches tend to end up dividing Aulén's 'objective' metaphor up into more than one category. Colin Gunton, for instance, separates it into a legal metaphor and a sacrificial metaphor. At the end of this development stands a book by John McIntyre, who lists thirteen different 'models' of salvation in the New Testament and Christian history. (Indeed, I listened to a paper at a conference recently from someone who had made a list of every different word he had ever found applied to the work of Jesus. Of course, many of them appeared to be different ways of saying the same thing, but he had reached a list of well over a hundred different words.)

It seems to me that we should at least pause briefly with these very 'narrow' metaphor schemes, and be aware of all the different language and imagery used to describe the cross. We might later want to start to group them together to make sense of the profusion of pictures, but there is always a danger in doing that too quickly. The danger is the possibility of grouping together things that are actually different. I have suggested earlier in the book that Aulén did this in developing his 'classic' theory, and that both critics and supporters of penal substitution have done it in recent years (critics in reading Anselm's work as a version of penal substitution; supporters in reading a lot of biblical and early church language of sacrifice or ransom as penal).

The attractions of lumping different ideas together like this are clear. If I happened to believe that only one theory of the atonement is right, I would like to find that theory in the biblical texts and all across the history of the church. Charles Hodge thinks his version of penal substitution is 'that which has been for ages regarded as the orthodox doctrine . . . common to the Latin, Lutheran and Reformed churches . . .' He can think this only by collapsing some fairly diverse pictures into the same category, but he has a lot invested in doing so, as it greatly strengthens his claim that his doctrine is right and all others wrong.

There are family resemblances, which I have tried to acknowledge in the earlier chapters. Everything that Aulén lumped together as 'objective' doctrine, from biblical accounts of sacrifice through Anselm to Calvin and Hodge and the evangelicals, clearly has something in common. They also have differences, however, and this is important. (In the recent debates it is important because there are several authors that seem to think that if they can criticise Hodge successfully, then they have destroyed every version of penal substitution, and Anselm's satisfaction theory with it. It's just not true.) It makes sense to group together different metaphors with others that they are similar to, so long as we always remember that they are different pictures, similar to each other, but not the same.

Judging the Metaphors

Metaphors communicate by comparing one thing to another. The comparison is always inexact, but nonetheless helpful because it takes something unknown and compares it to something known. At best, a metaphor is vivid, striking, arresting; it forces a new understanding, or an emotional response, because of this. At worst, a metaphor is a tired cliché, multiplying words without adding any understanding. Or it might be simply misleading or inappropriate, a bad comparison, and so a failure to communicate. Metaphors of the atonement, stories of salvation, are also going to be inexact. In every case there will be aspects of salvation they fail to communicate, as well as aspects they illuminate sharply. At best, they can grab the attention and the emotions; at worst, they will dull or confuse the mind.

Some metaphors become indispensable, because they describe something that we have no other grasp of. Scientists talk about very small particles as sometimes behaving as if they were waves, and at other times as if they were particles ('wave-particle duality'). We don't know what they are, these strange objects that can bounce like a football one moment and weave through a grating like a water wave the next. The metaphors remind us of the two aspects of their reality. Or we describe wine as dry, which it rather obviously isn't, because that metaphor has become useful to capture a taste sensation for which we have no better word.

If it is true that the atonement is something so fundamental that we can talk about it only by using pictures or metaphors drawn from more familiar, but less real, aspects of existence, like money or law or sacrifice, then how do we decide which pictures help and which get in the way? How do we decide which metaphors communicate well, and which are inappropriate and so obscure the truth? What criteria can we use to decide?

The answer must be: *revelation*. The descriptions of the cross in the Bible have a special place. It is not that we have to use them and only them – they, too, worked because they communicated successfully in their culture, but in my (Western) culture they might not help. Most Westerners, after all, have never seen an animal sacrificed, or a slave freed. But we have to work at trying to understand what it was that those metaphors communicated, and judge any new metaphors we might find by how well they, in turn, communicate the same things.

What did the Metaphors Communicate?

One of the things the biblical pictures point to is the *cost of salvation*. Or rather, they attempt to explain *why* salvation costs. If we assume, as surely we have to, that Jesus didn't die unnecessarily, then, somehow, our salvation depended on his death. And so the biblical writers get to work: a ransom, a sacrifice, a redemption price – in different ways, each picture is attempting to tell a story of how freedom or forgiveness or salvation does not come freely but costs. The cost is paid by another in each case, to set me free, but still, there is a cost, an awesome cost, the life of my Lord Jesus, and we need ways to begin to get hold of that. And so through the history of the church, early accounts of a ransom paid to the devil, or to God, and Anselm's account of a satisfaction made, and Calvin's account of penal substitution, are each ways of explaining the price that was paid.

Another feature of the biblical pictures is that each gives some understanding of *why we needed saving*. We were enslaved (but who to – the Law (Gal. 4), or sin (Rom. 6), the fear of death (Heb. 2:15), or the devil?), and Christ, by dying, set us free. We were far from God, and Christ, by dying as a sacrifice, brought us back. We were captives (but again: who to?), and Christ, by dying, paid our ransom. And so on.

If, however, all the different images of a price that needed paying point the same way, all these pictures also point in different directions. St Anselm asked us to consider how serious a thing sin is; the witness of the New Testament stories of salvation would seem to be that there is no end to the different ways in which sin has ruined and damaged us, and so the salvation Christ won for us meets a thousand different needs as every aspect of our lives and relationships are transformed.

At the end of the most recent film of the sinking of the *Titanic*, an old woman, Rose, remembers the events of the voyage and comments about her lover and rescuer, Jack: 'He saved me in every way that a person can be saved.' This sums up the love story that is, for that film, the solution to the basic problem faced by all films about the Titanic: how to fill the hour or so before the boat starts to sink. It may be a bit dated now, but at the time it was a pretty good line for beginning to talk about the work of Christ.

There are many other aspects to the New Testament witness, of course. Our theology of atonement ought to be able to give some account of the broader narrative: the incarnation, and the years of Christ's life, as well as the passion and the hours of his death; and the resurrection and ascension as well.

More than that, though, we might ask if our theology can cope with the details of the narrative. Jesus dies a particularly brutal, painful, shameful public death; and this must have been necessary, or his Father would have spared him it. As a friend of mine once put it, why could he not have died peacefully in the 'Jerusalem home for retired prophets'? It's a really good question, worth putting to any account of atonement.

A good atonement theology should recognise the Jewish character of everything that was going on and that made sense in that culture, and in terms of the Old Testament prophecies.

It should also give a decent account of the moral transformation of believers, make sense of our sanctification – our growth into holiness – as well as of our justification – the forgiveness of our sins.

A good atonement theology must picture the relationship between Jesus, his Father, and the Holy Spirit properly, not dividing the Trinity, nor ignoring the truth of it.

And it ought to speak to the scandal of structural sins, challenging oppression and prejudice and injustice in an obvious and prophetic way.

No doubt there are other conditions as well.

Alongside all this, our account of the atonement must make some sort of sense in whatever modern culture we find ourselves in. The pictures we draw must use symbols and images that people will recognise; the stories we tell must make sense. For academic theologians this is not quite so important: they can study the culture of Anselm's day, and so work out how his theory made sense. But for preachers and evangelists – and that means every Christian – it is vital. When announcing the saving death of Jesus to people in ringing tones from a pulpit, or explaining it in hesitant conversation over a coffee, we need to be able to tell stories of salvation that will communicate, that will connect with the people we are talking to.

This might seem a very tall order, but if we accept the need for – and legitimacy of – many metaphors, we do not need to find one theory, one picture, one story, that will meet all these conditions. Instead, we can tell many stories, which between them build up into a cohesive, coherent picture. Some of them will underplay, or miss completely, this or that aspect of the biblical witness; some will be easy to grasp in our culture, others difficult and will require additional explanation. But between them all, we will build up a composite picture of all that Jesus has done, a picture that will begin – but probably only begin – to be adequate to explain the wondrous cross.

The question, then, that I want to put with regard to penal substitution as a way of picturing the atonement is not: 'Does it answer everything?' but rather: 'Does it illuminate some things?' Does it help, alongside other stories, to build up a picture of the cross? Of course it has weaknesses – every metaphor does – but do its strengths counterbalance its weaknesses? Is there some aspect of the work of Jesus that, in our particular culture, it enables us to speak meaningfully of, some aspect that is missed by most or all of the other things we could say or stories we could tell?

If the answer to these questions is 'yes', then penal substitution may – and must – remain as one of our stories of salvation, balanced by others of course, but an important part nonetheless of our witness to the cross.

These questions form the substance of the next chapter.

Seven

'Sovereign One Who Died'

Exploring Penal Substitution

Should he who gave us breath and life
Be slaughtered for us all?

(Mark Altrogge, 'We Sing Your Mercies'
©1997 Sovereign Grace Praise, Copycare)

An Unacceptable Story?

Amongst the many stories of salvation told by Christian people down the ages is one that has come to be called penal substitution. This story is set in a law court, with sinners in the dock. The law stands against them, majestic and implacable, and there is no doubt of their guilt before it. The law demands punishment, and the law cannot be set aside. The punishment is death. Then, from nowhere, one steps forward. Innocent himself, he declares his solidarity with the sinners. In a marvellous exchange, he takes all their guilt to himself and clothes them in his righteousness. They, astonished, walk free from the court, having received a wonderful gift they did not request and did nothing to deserve, while he is led to the gallows to die.

This, in barest outline, is the story told by penal substitution.

But it is, thus stated, clearly an unacceptable story. Even on its own terms, the logic of the law court demands that guilt and punishment cannot be transferred like that. I might give a convicted criminal the money to pay her fine, if the offence is that minor, but I cannot do her community service, serve her prison sentence – and in countries where the death penalty is still imposed, I could not die in her place.

Theologically, there are more problems: God seems to have been replaced, or overshadowed, by an impersonal law; the deity of Christ is ignored completely; there is no place for the Holy Spirit, or the resurrection, or the church, or the moral transformation of believers. There is no explicit mention of mercy, grace, or love – the great truths of the gospel.

However, every story of salvation we might tell will have similar problems, if we tell it in such bald outline. Even if we stay with the basic biblical metaphors, in what sense is the death of Jesus an acceptable sacrifice to God, or an appropriate ransom payment (and to whom)? How does the deity of Christ, or the work of the Spirit, make a difference to the sacrifice, or the ransom?

We can do two things with these various metaphors: we can use them quickly, as passing illustrations to make a single point ('Jesus had to die so we could be freed from our sins – like the sacrificial animals needed to be killed . . .'), or we can attempt to tell a convincing and coherent story, as Hebrews does with sacrifice, perhaps.

What we can't do is take the quick illustration and pretend it is a fully worked out theory.

Yet many criticisms of penal substitution seem to do just that: take a quick sketch and criticise it as if it were a complete theology. It is not difficult to find tracts, sermons, anecdotes, and (especially) websites that offer accounts of penal substitution that are either ridiculous, abhorrent, or both. This is, of course, not interesting in itself – the same might be said of the doctrine of the Trinity, or the incarnation. (I approach Trinity Sunday each year, with great trepidation, expecting to hear one of the great truths of the Christian faith mangled horribly. I don't often recall being pleasantly surprised . . .). The fact that there are many, many poor statements of the doctrine is not a reason to criticise careful statements – indeed, it might be a reason to emphasise them.

In a moment I will try to offer a convincing account of penal substitution. But before I do, I want to stress that this, too, will be a partial and inadequate account of the atonement. As I argued in the previous chapter, all of our accounts of the atonement are of necessity always only partial and inadequate; and this one is no different. These partial and inadequate accounts, however, are all we have, and are enough to help us to grasp the wonderful reality of all that God has done for us in the death and resurrection of Christ. In narrating penal substitution, or indeed any other story of salvation, there will be rough edges, difficult logical gaps, and so on. But there will also, I hope and trust, be a glimpse of profound truth, and this makes living with the rest worthwhile.

The key insight for moving from the obviously inadequate story that I began with to a more adequate account is to recognise that many of the problems are one another's solutions. If, for instance, we address the problem that little or nothing is said about God, we will find that telling the story with more attention to the place of God in it will solve some of the other issues.

But enough introduction . . .

God and the Law

The story is still set in a law court – it would not be 'penal' if it were not. Where, then, is God? Since the story is controlled by the law, which sets the rules under which everything else operates, then God must be somehow identified with the law – God is in charge, after all.

But *how* can God be identified with the law? Well, the Scriptures themselves present us with the same problem: clearly, God is in control, but at times it seems there is a law, a standard, by which God himself may be judged. So, for instance, Abraham can ask, 'Will not the judge of all the earth do right?' and expect (and even demand) a positive answer. God will do right; God will act rightly, lovingly; God will be good and just – if he did not, if he were not, he would not be God.

The law, then, is God's character, or at least an aspect of it. The one of whom Scripture declares, 'Your eyes are too pure to look on evil' (Hab. 1:13) cannot simply ignore or pass over sin, evil, wrong-doing. This, indeed, is the whole point of Habakkuk's comment. The prophet is complaining that God is apparently ignoring, or even approving of, the evil that the Babylonians are doing. The essence of his complaint is that God is not being true to himself.

God's answer, of course, is that his justice will be displayed in time, and that until then, 'The righteous will live by faith' (Hab. 2:4). God does not respond to Habakkuk by saying that his complaint is misguided, that pleading the righteousness of God's own character against God's actions is inappropriate; instead, he accepts the prophet's point. Because of who he is, God will do what is just and right. And if it is just and right that sin, rebellion against God, must be dealt with, punished, then God will do that, because of who he is. To see the terrible and implacable law standing against the sinner as an aspect of who God is, then, is entirely appropriate and biblical. Our God is jealous (Ex. 34:14), and his holiness is a consuming fire (Is. 33:14). It remains an awesome, terrible thing to fall into the hands of the living God (Heb. 10:31).

We cannot stop here, however. It is not just that God's jealous holiness stands against the sinner. God is not just the law in the courtroom – that would be too impersonal a picture. God is also the judge. God acts to uphold his perfection. When sin or evil or pollution comes before him, it is destroyed. When Achan, son of Carmi, disobeyed the Lord's command, God's judgement fell (Josh. 7); when Ananias and Sapphira lied before God, fire consumed them (Acts 5). At the end of time, Jesus tells us, the nations will be gathered before him, and he will judge them on the basis of the works of mercy they have or haven't done (Mt. 25:31–46), inflicting punishment – eternal punishment – on those judged guilty (Mt. 25:46). God – Father, Son and Holy Spirit – will pass judgement to uphold his law.

This, however, is not the whole truth; it is not even the most important part of the truth – indeed it *can't* be, or the story I told in the beginning would end the way law court stories so often do, with a conviction and the judge saying, 'Take him down!' with grim relish.

One of the most astonishing passages in the Scriptures is set in a courtroom, this time with God playing the prosecuting council.

In Hosea 11, God speaks of Israel as his son. The first verse sets the tone: God has loved Israel; Israel has rejected God. Israel is a rebellious and obstinate son. God has disciplined Israel, but it has done no good. And we are, I think, meant to see here references back to the law in Deuteronomy, where an obstinate and rebellious son is to be brought before the city elders and sentenced to death by stoning (Deut. 21:18–21). This will 'purge the evil from among you' (Deut. 21:21), according to that law. And so Hosea sets up the court. God is the parent, bringing a rebellious son to judgement. God announces Israel's crimes and failures, and the inevitable punishment that will come (Hos. 11:5–6).

But then there is a break in the story. God will not do it. The law demands punishment, demands it so that evil can be purged and the community restored to being what it should be, but God will not accept his own law. 'How can I give you up? How can I hand you over?' asks God (Hos. 11:8), and this compassion wins the day. Why? 'Because I am God, not human, the Holy One amongst you' (Hos. 11:9). Because of who God is, because of God's holiness, mercy will triumph over anger, and compassion displace judgement. God's holiness is indeed a consuming fire, but it is the consuming fire of his love.

As I pointed out in chapter five, this same insight was part of John Calvin's account of penal substitution, the first and classic telling of this story. The first word must be God's love, grace and mercy, or else there would be no atonement for us to argue about. 'This is love . . . God loved us and sent his Son as an atoning sacrifice for our sins' (1 Jn. 4:10). If, in the picture of the courtroom, God's holy character is the law against which we are judged, and God himself is the judge who passes sentence, God is also the reason the trial takes an unexpected turn, because God's love and mercy will not let the normal legal processes follow their course.

I have already commented that there are some very bad accounts of penal substitution out there. One common feature in bad accounts is that of trying to separate, or divide, God. The Father becomes the implacable judge, upholding the law and demanding punishment, and the Son the loving Saviour who turns aside the demanded suffering. Not only is this extraordinarily bad theology – Father, Son and Spirit always act together, never in opposition to one another – it is also very unbiblical. In Hosea it is the Father who will not carry through the demands of the law; in Matthew 25 Jesus passes judgement without any qualms.

How, then, should we continue to tell the story?

One way would be to tell it as a fight against the law. If we just followed Hosea, we could see the law as some evil power that held us captive, and see God's action as some sort of daring jail break, liberating the (admittedly guilty) prisoners. The story of salvation would then be simple: God fought the law, and the law lost. Martin Luther tended towards this view sometimes, and it is another interesting and suggestive story of salvation. I preach the cross in these terms, sometimes, particularly when addressing young people who have grown up evangelical and who have often heard so much from well-meaning youth leaders about what they should and shouldn't do that the message of God's grace was rather lost. To hear that what God does in Jesus is to tear up the rulebook because he loves us too much to let it get in the way, can be immensely liberating for these people.

That is not penal substitution, however. If we retain the insights – serious, biblical insights – that the law is an expression of God's own character, and that God is the judge who upholds the law, but then add the great truth of God's love in, how might the story go?

Law and Love

God will not tear up the rulebook, because the rulebook is his. It is an expression of his character, of his love. Always in the Bible, law follows after love.

The Ten Commandments begin, 'I am the Lord your God, who brought you up out of the land of Egypt out of the place of slavery; you shall have no other gods before me.' God has saved, has loved, and now guides and instructs us on how best to use our new-found freedom so that we do not damage ourselves anymore.

Paul's letters almost all follow the same shape: a long account of how God has saved us in Jesus, followed, in effect, by 'Therefore, live like this . . .' (Rom. 12:1; Eph. 4:1; Phil. 2:12; Col. 2:16; etc.). God loves us, acts to save and redeem us, and then, and only then, and still out of love, begins to show us how to live. The law, too, is a gift of God's love.

But precisely because of this, breaking the law matters. It is not a breach of some arbitrary and meaningless limit, but an act that distorts and pollutes and damages us, and the community we are a part of, and the whole of creation. Somehow, that damage must be repaired; the law must be upheld, and so judgement, and punishment, must come. As in Deuteronomy 21:25, the role of punishment is that 'evil may be purged', that damage may be restored. It, too, is an expression of God's love.

So God will not tear up the rulebook. The accused stands in the dock, and the guilty verdict is inevitable.

But must punishment follow the verdict? Can God not then exercise clemency, and simply forgive the offenders? St Anselm answered this question by announcing, 'You have not considered how serious a thing sin is.'

I am not sure this is a good answer: the question is not how serious a thing sin is, but whether it is more serious than God's desire to save his people. And the answer to that, necessarily, is no. So Anselm's answer works only if the seriousness of sin places some sort of necessity on God. There must be some good reason why God cannot, whilst remaining true to himself, simply declare the offender guilty and then forgive, refusing to impose any punishment.

What might this reason be?

There are two good answers to this question. The first is to recall that penal substitution, like any story of salvation, is an attempt to understand how Christ actually saved us. And Christ's salvation was costly. It involved unspeakable pain, public torture and shame. More, it involved Christ being identified with the cursed (Gal. 3:13), with the lawless (Is. 53:12), with sin itself (2 Cor. 5:21). This suffering and shame was not purposeless, a mere accident of history (Mt. 26:53–54); it happened for a reason. I do not think we can ever fully understand that reason, the logic that links Christ's sufferings with our salvation; that is why we need pictures, metaphors, stories of salvation. And one of the things we do with those pictures and stories is recall ways in which pain and suffering and shame can result in good. A sacrifice, or a ransom – or a punishment which, when it is fulfilled, leaves the offender free. None of the analogies are exact, but they are important because they try to comprehend the facts of what Jesus did. On this answer we might not know *why* punishment, or sacrifice, or ransom, or some other payment, was necessary, but we can know *that* it was, because Jesus in fact died for us.

A second answer goes back to the law, which of course was given and established by God. In Deuteronomy 25, which refers to the law about the rebellious child that I have already mentioned in this chapter, the death of the offender removes the evil from the community. This is fairly easy to understand, but the wider law gets more complicated. There is a sense in which sin, even unknown, unintentional sin, pollutes the community, and indeed the land. The punishment of known, intentional wrong-doing, and sacrifice for other sins, becomes a way of removing this pollution, pollution which, if left unchecked, will eventually destroy the community. The land itself will evict the people if the pollution gets too great (Leviticus 18:28 speaks of the land 'vom-iting out' the people). The picture here is perhaps of a moral order which cannot be violated. We cannot pretend that a river is not polluted if it is, and the same is true of a society.

Pollution is, of course, only one more metaphor or picture – but again, that is all we have. (We could use more technical-sounding words, like miasma, but I am not sure they would do anything more than hide the fact that this is still just another metaphor.) Somehow, there is a pollution, a corruption, damage done by wrongdoing, which must be put right. One way of think-ing about this, a way invited by the law itself, is to think of the punishment of sin as a means of clearing the pollution, restoring the corruption, repairing the damage. So, when we tell the story in terms of penal substitution, part of the story is that God cannot simply forgive those who are guilty – there is a need for punish-ment to be enacted. Otherwise, the damage would remain unre-paired, the pollution uncleansed.

So . . . the accused stand in the dock; the guilty verdict is pro-nounced. The only possible punishment under the law is death. The God who is love, however, will not allow the sentence to fall. As Hosea prophesied, as Anselm and Calvin understood and taught in their different ways, this is the key reality of any account of the atonement. And so God takes the punishment on himself. And once the punishment has fallen, those in the dock are free to go, saved now from all that stood against them and demanded their death . . . We are free to go.

It seems to me that the key insight of any account of penal sub-stitution is precisely this: God takes the due punishment on him-self. The great Swiss-German theologian Karl Barth saw this as the very heart of the gospel (indeed, of who God is), arguing that God chooses death, rejection, suffering for himself, and life and hope and salvation for us.

The picture needs to become more complicated, as I will show in a moment, with an account of the incarnation, and so the spe-cific suffering of God the Son as a human being. But as I said before in connection with the identity of the judge, we cannot divide God up into an angry Father, a loving Son (and a forgot-ten and inactive Spirit, it seems . . .). I know that plenty of pre-sentations of penal substitution do this, and that just makes them bad presentations. Calvin didn't. Charles Hodge didn't. In more recent times J.I. Packer and John Stott didn't (indeed, Stott says that any such idea must be 'repudiated with the utmost vehe-mence'). Penal substitution in its classical, most careful, and most influentially stated form, does not make this mistake. If it did, it would be indefensible, as far as I can see. We cannot tell stories about an angry God and a loving saviour without being false to the Scripture and the gospel. The story that must be told is that punishment is due, and that the holy, loving God takes it upon himself.

The Justice of God

The question, though, is how can he? Justice does not allow a transfer of punishment from one person to another, as we all know. This is perhaps the most serious criticism of penal substi-tution as a story of salvation: it depends upon something funda-mentally unjust, despite claiming to be an account based on a consideration of justice. How, then, can it be a helpful or useful way of talking about the cross?

Some of the classic answers to this question are not very helpful. John Calvin simply points to the Old Testament sacrifices, particu-larly to the scapegoat at the Day of Atonement, and claims that here we see guilt transferred from one being to another, so clearly it is something that can happen. I suspect that Calvin is here reading rather more into the sacrificial texts than can be proved by strict exegesis. I also don't find the response particularly helpful. Even if he is just right about the sacrifices, the upholding of justice is so central to any account of penal substitution that invoking something so straightforwardly unjust would make this an impossible story. It descends to the level of misleading or inappropriate metaphor, best discarded and forgotten. If we are to continue to use penal substitution as a picture of salvation, we need a better answer to this problem.

Charles Hodge distinguishes between two different senses of the word *guilt*. In English, *guilt* refers both to the psychological state of being conscious of wrongdoing, and to the legal state of being liable for punishment. When Daniel refused to obey King Darius's command not to pray to God (Dan. 6), he was faced with a choice between obeying the law, but doing something he knew to be wrong, and doing what is right, but breaking the law. He chose, of course, the second way, and he became guilty in the second sense, but not in the first; on the other hand, obedience to the King would have made him guilty in the first sense but not in the second. Hodge wants to claim that guilt in the first sense cannot be transferred, but that guilt in the second sense can. With God's perfect law in view, our sins make us guilty in both senses, but the first sense, an awareness of our own failings, demands humility and repentance from us; the second sense, liability to punishment through legal failure, can, Hodge thinks, be transferred to Christ. Hodge perhaps assumes this too readily, but I think his point is worth thinking about: if we can distinguish between these two senses of guilt, then it is at least less unacceptable that guilt can be transferred from one person to another.

God's Identification With Us

I would like to offer a different way of understanding the story that penal substitution tells.

I have argued that the essence of the story is that God takes the due punishment on himself – but, of course, it is God the Son who dies, having become human like us. This is an important clue to how we should understand the question. I want to argue that God can take our guilt because he identifies so closely with us that our guilt *can* be shared, or transferred. Essentially, I want to argue for a notion of 'corporate responsibility'. *Corporate*, of course, comes from the Latin word *corpus*, which means 'body' (think 'corpse'!). Jesus, as the head of the body, is one with all the members of the body. He can bear the moral responsibility, the guilt, for their sin, and they can enjoy the moral responsibility, the reward, for his righteousness. (Phrased like this, it might sound as though Jesus died only for his body, the church, and not for the world. I will come back to that problem.)

In modern Western society we are generally unhappy with notions of corporate responsibility. In Britain there have been a few prosecutions under a new law allowing businesses or other bodies to be held responsible for deaths or negligence, and it has been interesting to hear how dissatisfied the victims are with these cases. They want someone – *a person* – held responsible: a fine, however swingeing, applied to the business does not satisfy their sense of justice. We might, I suppose, respond to this by pointing out that in the story of salvation that is penal substitution, one person is held responsible – Jesus – but I don't think that quite gets to the point. The problem seems to be a sense that someone, or perhaps several someones, did something wrong: a director chose to cut safety spending, or an inspector missed the crucial defect, or a worker was inattentive, overtired, drunk, or otherwise incompetent. For the firm alone to be punished means the people who are truly guilty go unpunished.

The demand, sometimes heard, that the managing director or other leader of the business be tried and punished is perhaps more relevant to the sort of corporate responsibility that I am trying to get at here. In criminal law this is not a well-developed idea, but it happens in politics (at least in Britain) from time to time. A cabinet minister will resign because something has gone on in her department which should not have; there is no suggestion that she was involved, or even knew about it, but it happened on her 'watch', so she is held responsible. (I believe a military officer can be held responsible for the actions of his or her men in a similar way.)

In (British) criminal law, the one place where this is becoming common is the family: it is now well established (if still controversial) that parents can be tried and punished for the failings of their children in various ways.

This idea is much more common in other societies, where punishment for wrongdoing might fall on any member of a family, clan, or village and still be regarded as just. The village is guilty, not the individual. There are even societies where the punishment for murder is the death of someone of similar social standing, so the actual murderer might be completely immune from punishment, it falling instead on one of his servants or elders. I do not want to argue that this is how justice should look, of course, but the realisation that the Western obsession with locating the particular offender is not the only way to think about justice might help us to enlarge our imaginations. We might then begin to imagine that it could be just for punishment for the faults of the members of the body to fall on the head of the body.

The classical biblical example, of course, is Paul's contrast in Romans 5 between sin and death coming to us all through Adam's failure, and life and justification coming to us all through Christ. The passage does not necessarily teach that guilt may be transferred or shared between Adam and us all, or between Christ and us all, but it certainly again invites us to imagine that this might be the case. More widely, Paul's great account of salvation is union with Jesus: the believer is 'in Christ', a phrase which again points to a close identification.

None of this finally proves that guilt can be transferred, but it doesn't need to: we are talking here about helpful and credible stories of salvation, not about completely worked through logical schemes. In being born as one of us, in baptism in the Jordan, in being made sin for us, God the Son identifies with us, so much so that, without injustice, he may bear our guilt and we may enjoy his blessedness. It is a marvellous exchange, which we cannot explain fully, but which we can begin to glimpse the possibility of.

Jesus, then, bears the punishment for us. The punishment is death, and so he goes to the cross and there dies. God suffers, in the person of the incarnate Son, so that we do not have to.

Of course, at no point in this story does the Father ever stop loving the Son (or, indeed, us), and so the resurrection is the almost inevitable consequence. For our salvation, the Son must die, but God will not let his Holy One see decay (Acts 13:35). Death understood as the process of dying is necessary, but death understood as staying dead is not, and so the Son rises on the third day.

What of us?

Well, we need to get to the question of who's the 'us' in this story, but first some other comments are necessary.

We are largely spectators to the story of salvation told by penal substitution. This is sometimes seen as a problem for the tradition, because our theology of atonement ought to talk about our lives being transformed, and about reasons and resources for holy living. Indeed it ought, but I still believe that the Reformation insight of separating justification (the fact of our salvation in the free gift of God) from sanctification (the working out of our salvation in our lives) was a good one. It protects against the mistake of thinking that God saves us because we do good things. It stops us from trying to earn our way to heaven, which seems to be a natural human instinct.

Of course I want to say that both justification and sanctification are gifts God gives us through the cross of Jesus, and that God never gives one without the other, so that everyone who is saved will set out on a path of growth in holiness and love. But there is some value in having some (not all!) of our stories of salvation in which we are essentially bystanders. These stories protect one great truth: that Jesus saves us regardless of what we have done, that the worst sinner is welcome without doing one thing first.

Now, alongside those stories we need some others – ones that talk of transformation, of being born again, of the work of the Spirit, and of the call to visible holiness and a serious discipleship that comes to all whom Jesus calls to be his own. The Lord's command, 'Be holy, as I am holy' must be heard. But it is not the only thing that must be heard. If we try to present penal substitution as saying everything that needs to be said about the cross, then it would be inadequate on this question. If, instead, we believe that we need many stories of salvation, then it is a benefit to have some – perhaps even only one – of them that hold on to the truth that in Jesus forgiveness comes full and free regardless of who we are. Other stories can be told of how we should follow, of how to live as peacemakers, and of the inescapably political nature of Christian discipleship; but let us tell at least one story for broken sinners that speaks of grace and not law, that offers hope without making demands . . . please?

Who Can be Saved?

So, then, who's the *us* in penal substitution?

A largely unhelpful debate has run through Protestant Christianity over the past three centuries over whether Jesus died for the whole world or for the church only. Some people have wanted to believe that it was just for the church (or just for the 'elect'), because it makes Jesus' salvation definite: he did not die in the mere *hope* that some might believe, be baptised into his death, and so come to salvation. No, he died specifically for each one who will be found in heaven – there is no 'perhaps', no failure associated with the death of Jesus. This is obviously attractive. But the loss of not being able to say that it was for the world, the whole world, that Jesus died, that every aspect, every inch, every moment of the whole of creation is transformed decisively by this astonishing thing that has happened . . . this is an enormous loss, quite apart from the seemingly clear teaching of Scripture that 'God so loved the world . . .'

I want to say that both are true. I want some of the pictures we paint, some of the stories of salvation we tell, to hold each of these precious truths. When we tell a story that sounds like penal substitution, we celebrate the power of God's salvation, which cannot be broken, and so which is unquestionably definite. In this story the *us* in penal substitution is the church, the body of Christ, the people for whom Christ's death is visibly and unquestionably transformative.

But then there are also other stories that we need to tell, stories that give us different perspectives, different aspects, of the awesome thing that God has done for us, that will point to the potential transformation – or even the actual transformation – of the whole world.

My contention then is that, properly told, penal substitution is a story that helps us make sense of the cross of Christ, of the astonishing thing that happened at Calvary. But it is not the *only* way of describing the cross – not even a privileged one. It can't be either of these things if what I said in the previous chapter about metaphors and stories was even nearly right. However, penal substitution is a way of talking that we should hold on to, because it preserves certain truths that are taught better by telling this story than by telling any other story I have ever heard.

In the last chapter I want to turn to those things that are actually important: to Christian discipleship, and to preaching, and to worship, and to Christians caring for one another in the church and caring for all those outside the church. I want to ask, very simply, how penal substitution might help in these contexts.

Before I do that, however, I am going to look again at some criticisms of penal substitution. I wanted in this book to talk positively about how Jesus has saved us, not ignoring criticisms, but answering them quietly along the way by telling the story properly, so that it was not vulnerable to this or that criticism. But the controversy cannot be ignored: people have claimed that this way of talking is both theologically wrong and culturally unhelpful. We need to ask, are they right?

Eight

'Overwhelmed by the Mystery'

Criticisms of Penal Substitution

'You came into a world of shame,
And paid the price I could not pay.'

(Matt Redman, 'For the Cross')

Stories That Connect

A preacher preparing an evangelistic sermon. A church leader invited to lead a meditation around the cross on Good Friday. A university student asked one night in halls why Christians are so interested in Jesus' death. A youth leader whose young people ask why the cross matters. A parent, at the school gate, asked why she is a Christian . . .

All these people need to be able to tell a story of salvation. They need some picture of the cross that will make sense to their hearers. We have failed, far too often, in modern Britain to tell stories of salvation that do make sense to our hearers. Sometimes the stories make no sense at all. We gabble some half-understood gospel presentation from an ancient tract, not really believing it ourselves. Sometimes the stories might make some sense, but there is no chance of their being heard or understood by the people we tell them to.

I used to help out in a youth mission in inner London, where they told volunteers a tale of how not to relate to the young people. One summer some university students had come to help, and one earnest young man had gone into one of the clubs and begun to talk to the young people, and within a minute was punched so hard he hit the floor. The lad who punched him was pulled out, and when asked why, announced, 'He said I smelt!' This confused the folk who ran the clubs, so they asked the student what he'd been saying and received the reply, 'I just asked him if he was a Christian.' This still made little sense, so they pressed him: What exactly had he said? 'I asked if he'd been washed in the blood . . .'

Hugh MacDiarmid, the greatest Scots poet of the twentieth century, once wrote that ministers, along with other communicators, were 'living like maggots on dead words'. MacDiarmid was no friend of Christianity, but his diagnosis was spot on. We need stories of salvation that are not decomposed, but that make sense to our culture. Ways of picturing what Jesus did on the cross that will attract and interest and excite teenagers in Southwark and New York and Delhi and Dubai and everywhere else, not confuse and enrage them.

I was at the Scottish Baptist Assembly recently, enjoying an all-age service led by Fischy Music, a Christian group who do a lot of good work in schools. They told us about discovering that almost every teacher in Scotland thought the biggest problem for children was bullying, and how in response they had written a song about Jesus facing up to the bullies – the Pharisees, of course, but also the tempter in the desert, and on the cross. If we really want to unpick it theologically, they were telling a story of salvation which echoed Gustav Aulén's account of Christ winning the victory, but they were doing it in a way that connected directly with the felt need of children.

That's what we need: stories of salvation that mean something today, in the cultures and contexts in which we find ourselves.

And the question is, can penal substitution be such a story? It may be a meaningful way of talking about what happened at Calvary if properly understood, but that is not yet enough. Anselm's account of satisfaction connected with a feudal society which understood and believed in the overriding duty of fealty to an overlord. The old Greek 'physicalist' idea connected to people who assumed some other old Greek ideas about human nature. Neither of these, however, is useful for the preacher or the youth leader or the parent I began this chapter with. They are important ideas in the classroom, when someone studies theology, because they enlarge our vision of what the cross might be about. But they are no longer preachable. They are built on dead words. They no longer connect. Is it the same with penal substitution?

I want, in this chapter, to address criticisms of penal substitution. There are two sets of criticisms that need to be faced. On the one hand, there is the question of whether penal substitution is a good story to tell about the cross – whether as a metaphor it succeeds in illuminating more than it obscures and in illuminating some truths that are not to be found elsewhere. On the other hand, there is the question of cultural relevance, the question I have just been opening up. Both sorts of criticisms have been raised in the recent debates. Penal substitution was, for Protestants at least, a dominant story of salvation between 1600 and 1800. Was this a mistake, was it always a caricature of the cross? Or was it appropriate, a story that connected with that culture, but one which now, because of cultural change, needs to be relegated to the history books as we look for something better?

Theological Criticisms: Violence, Abuse and Hypocrisy

Redemptive violence?

'The myth of redemptive violence' is a phrase heard a lot in some church circles these days, and it perhaps needs to be thought about a bit more carefully than it sometimes is.

The phrase was invented by Walter Wink, who got the idea from the French philosopher René Girard. Girard acknowledges openly that if his ideas are right then bits, at least, of the Bible don't make very much sense. Nonetheless, at heart the phrase captures something that many of us will feel the truth of. Our culture is addicted to stories of salvation through violence. Westerns are not as popular at the cinema as they once were, but provide perhaps the classic example: all will be put right through a climactic gun battle (ideally with John Wayne on the winning side . . .). Or we have James Bond meeting the baddie in a kill-or-be-killed confrontation, and Arnold Schwarzenegger once, and Bruce Willis still, doing the same. Even when there are tales of redemption (think of Darth Vader in the *Star Wars* series), still, violence will solve the problem (Vader's redemption allows him to kill the Emperor).

Perhaps different nations have learnt the story through their histories of war: Britain forged much of its self-identity by remembering when it stood defiant and alone against the military might of dictators such as Napoleon and Hitler and – against all the odds – won. The history is told with a fair bit of spin, of course (Napoleon, Hitler, and pretty much every other would-be conqueror of Europe were defeated largely by the Russian winter . . .), but it is important nonetheless.

As I was finishing this book one of my American students asked me: 'What's with the poppies?' He was aware that a ritual of enormous cultural significance was going on, but could find no explanation. For anyone not British, the selling and wearing of poppies, and the keeping of a two-minute silence, on November 11 (the date the First World War ended) to remember those who died in war is an almost universal national observance. Indeed, this year a broadcaster, Jon Snow, was castigated and vilified across the press for daring to ask whether the wearing of a poppy should be compulsory for anyone appearing on television.

Whether the connection between war and identity is the reason or not, we have, deep in our culture, a belief that violence can provide the final solutions to problems and issues.

Twenty years ago our political leaders declared a 'war on drugs'; five years ago it was a 'war on terror'. Drugs and terrorism are, of course, enormously significant (and closely linked) issues that urgently need to be dealt with, and probably at least some of the policies embarked on in these two 'wars' have been beneficial, but the choice of the war metaphor is still revealing: when faced with an intractable problem, we look to violence to redeem us.

I do not want here to get into the argument of whether Christians should be pacifists, but the notion that violence can ever be a good solution to a problem is one all Christians will resist. Even at the most violent parts of the Old Testament, when it seems God has sponsored war (and indeed genocide) as the people of Israel invade the land of Canaan to destroy and kill everything they find there at God's express instruction (Josh. 8:1–2, etc.), still it is clear that the war is morally dubious; so when Joshua sees the Lord and asks, 'Are you with us, or with our enemies?' the answer is 'Neither . . .' (Josh. 6:13–14). And when Jesus comes, he conquers not by military might and violence, but by loving and dying.

(Being somewhat behind the times, I have just watched Peter Jackson's *Lord of the Rings* films for the first time. The story there is that the ultimate weapon of war – the Ring of Power – is available, but must not be used, because it will finally destroy and corrupt all who use it. The constant temptation to seize an easy, violent solution is to be resisted, and the war will be won by destroying, not deploying, the ultimate weapon. Hobbits can carry the Ring better than most because they, uniquely among the races of Middle Earth, are not disposed to warfare as an answer to their troubles. My sense was that the films stressed the significance of the various battles fought rather more than the books did. Tolkien, of course, described his work as 'fundamentally religious and Catholic'.)

Does penal substitution pervert all this? Does it exalt violence? As far as I can see the answer must be 'no'.

The Violence of the Cross

If we improperly separate the Father and the Son, if we forget that Jesus is God just as truly as the Father is God, then we might see it as a story of a vengeful God who demands that violence be inflicted – but of course at that point we have left anything like Christianity way behind, and so what we are saying is irrelevant anyway. The cross was a violent event: for all its (many) faults, Mel Gibson's *The Passion of the Christ* at least made that clear. Any account of the cross we offer is going to need to make sense of that violence. The worst thing we can do is assume it wasn't necessary or important. Then we would be saying that God put his Son through all the humiliation and torture and shame unnecessarily, that the Father's answer to the anguished prayer of Gethsemane was, 'Actually, there's lots of other ways we could do this, but I'm sticking with this one.' That really would be an unworthy story to tell of God.

So we tell stories about sacrifices, or ransoms, or battles with demons, or indeed legal executions, as a way of trying to understand why the violence was necessary. And in every case the answer is the same, more or less: God has so ordered the world that the inevitable consequence of sin is violence, suffering and death; and rather than let *us* suffer these things, God takes them on himself. Penal substitution says nothing more than this. It does not support, or legitimate, let alone give rise to, 'the myth of redemptive violence'. (My sense from what I know of the preaching of the Crusades is that accounts of Christ's struggle with, and victory over, the evil powers are far more likely to do that.)

The cross as child abuse?

The comment that provided the occasion for the most recent arguments about the cross in British evangelicalism was the suggestion that the cross, understood as penal substitution, is 'a form of cosmic child abuse'. It was a throwaway line in a generally very good book, but to people who held penal substitution to be an important biblical truth it was (perhaps understandably) incendiary.

The idea was not original: it comes from some American 'Feminist Theologians' – I think very first from Rita Nakashima Brock in 1989. (Feminist Theology is a recognised school of theology. These days it is, of course, possible – easy, in fact – to be a feminist without signing up to Feminist Theology.) Here it was a specific form of a general set of discussions about the way Christian atonement theology legitimises violence and encourages victims of violence to accept their abuse.

The general idea was that any account of the cross that accepted that God wanted or needed someone to suffer and die does at least three things: (i) it makes violence acceptable (since God did/does it himself!); (ii) it disempowers victims (who are encouraged to suffer patiently as Jesus suffered patiently); and (iii), when linked to Father-Son language, it makes it look as if the core of the gospel story is an act of child abuse leading to infanticide.

Such criticisms are, of course, extraordinarily serious if they are in any way valid. I want to make a several comments, however.

First, these criticisms were not directed initially at penal substitution, but at all Christian accounts of atonement indiscriminately.

It might be that they apply peculiarly strongly to penal substitution, but that is not obvious (at least to me). Take, for example, the basic biblical picture of sacrifice. Sacrifices are, by definition, offered to God. Now here is a story in which God really is pleased with the death of an innocent victim, far more so than in penal accounts. We cannot use such criticisms to object to penal substitution and then pretend that other stories of salvation are unaffected.

Second, these criticisms often read as if any story involving any violence anywhere is to be rejected. As I have just commented, however, there is violence at the heart of the Christian gospel. Jesus died brutally, on a cross. When doing Christian theology, we may argue about how to *explain* the violence, but not about the *fact* of it – as I pointed out in chapter three, there is not much New Testament left without the cross.

These are not yet good reasons for rejecting the criticisms (I am coming to those . . .), but I want anyone who accepts the arguments to see just how much they destroy. If the arguments of these feminist theologians work, then there is little left by way of atonement theology. This particular bomb is powerful enough to destroy the whole building, not just the one room we don't like.

Answering the Critics

So, can the criticisms be answered?

I believe so: it seems to me they work both with an inadequate idea of sin, and with no understanding of the Trinity.

On the first, no serious Christian theology paints God as wanting violence or enjoying death; somehow, because of sin, such things just become necessary. God is like a surgeon operating on a cancer: a surgeon doesn't get a kick out of cutting bits out of people's bodies; she does it because there is no other way to heal and save the patient. Just so, atonement theology is built on the assertion that sin must be dealt with, or else we, the sinners, will be destroyed by it. Someone may, of course, disagree with this assertion (although Scripture, history and literature combine to make it almost incontrovertible); but to criticise Christian atonement theology as if this point were not assumed and asserted is just unfair.

Second, the criticisms that begin with the feminist theologians assume an improper separation between Father and Son (and no account of the Spirit, usually). If we do not realise that God is on the cross, that God is taking the suffering on himself, then we have not begun to understand what is going on. As Jesus said, 'I and the Father are one' (Jn. 10:30). The story is not of a vengeful Father punishing an innocent Son, but of a loving and holy God, Father, Son and Spirit, bearing himself the pain of our failures. (I am aware that some of the feminist theologians I am talking about would not accept any traditional account of the deity of Jesus, but in that case, of course, other theological positions don't work and need changing. If you pull away half the foundations, the building is likely to collapse . . .).

Now of course this does not mean that there are not presentations of penal substitution – or, indeed, of other accounts of the atonement – that are guilty of these failings; I am sure there are. I am sure, also, that some perfectly adequate accounts are misheard in these ways sometimes: every preacher knows that, however careful you are to avoid a particular misunderstanding, sometimes people hear you wrongly (and every preacher knows that sometimes God uses that wrong hearing for good – it keeps us humble, I suppose!). But a proper account of penal substitution is not vulnerable to these criticisms.

Forgiveness 'Full and Free'?

One last theological criticism, then: God commands us to forgive freely, up to seventy times seven; why, then, does he not do the same? Does not the idea that God needs some satisfaction, or that punishment must fall and sin cannot be simply forgiven, just make God a hypocrite? He expects us to forgive without expecting payment; why doesn't he?

The answer, of course, is that he does. In the previous chapter I noted that one of the other common criticisms of penal substitution is that it asks nothing of us – we are virtually bystanders in the story that I told. God – Father, Son and Spirit – does everything necessary. That is free forgiveness. God asks us to do nothing. We are just spectators – spectators from the dock, yes, but spectators still – as he does everything necessary that we might go free. Of course, in the story there is a cost, but it is a cost born by God himself.

So perhaps penal substitution teaches us something important about forgiveness: that it is not easy, painless, or cheap, but it costs and hurts. And God's call on us to forgive, to love our enemies, is not easy and cheap, but will cost us and hurt us. The call, though, is to live as God lived, to bear the cost and pain ourselves so that we demand nothing, but offer free forgiveness, to those who have wronged us.

Violent, abusive and hypocritical?

No, penal substitution, rightly understood, is a story of salvation that shows God's determination to deal with violence and sin, and to refuse to let it have the upper hand. It's a story that teaches us deep lessons about God's free forgiveness. Like Anselm's great account, it is a story that should not be forgotten within the church, because it profoundly illuminates aspects of what God did for us at Calvary.

Is the story at all relevant outside the church, however? Should it, like Anselm, be relegated to a useful bit of history, or can it still speak today? What of the cultural criticisms?

Cultural Criticisms

I have said a couple of times that penal substitution was the dominant way of talking about the cross for Protestant Christians between 1600 and 1800. This, of course, raises the question: What happened in 1800? Was it the shifting winds of theological fashion, or did something serious change, in the culture perhaps, that meant that this story no longer communicated as well as it had done?

It was indeed a time of great cultural change: in Vienna Ludwig van Beethoven performed and published his first symphony; in Britain Wordsworth and Coleridge had just published their *Lyrical Ballads*. The precise, logical, scientific eighteenth-century 'Enlightenment' was giving way to the passionate and exultant celebrations of Romanticism.

But cultural changes keep happening. Romantic passion gave way to *fin de siecle* ennui and to modernist pessimism, and then, in 1917, Marcel Duchamp smuggled a urinal into an art exhibition, signed it with a pseudonym, called it 'Fountain', and postmodernity had arrived (although it took some decades for most of us to notice . . .).

It is not the mere *fact* of cultural change that will make a particular account of the atonement unintelligible, but whether the change in culture affects the ideas on which that account depends.

Nonetheless, historically, there does seem to be good reason to look for something happening around 1800 which affected penal substitution. I have an idea about what it is, but let me first consider some cultural criticisms of penal substitution that have been significant recently.

One theme that can be found regularly is the notion that Britain, or the West, has changed from being a 'guilt' society to a 'shame' society, and penal substitution is no longer relevant, because it speaks to people who think themselves guilty, which no one does anymore.

The contrast between 'guilt societies' and 'shame societies' was conceived of and developed by social anthropologists in the middle of the twentieth century. Both guilt and shame, anthropologists claim, are mechanisms that develop in societies to ensure social control. A 'guilt' society seeks to develop an internal mechanism for social control in its citizens: knowing I have done wrong, I will judge myself and feel guilty. A 'shame' society relies on communal mechanisms of social control: if I have done wrong, I will be judged and shamed by my community.

In the case where I have done something wrong and everyone knows about it, the two systems might appear very similar, and the same applies in the case where I am an upright citizen and known to be so. If, however, I am falsely believed to have committed a crime, in a shame culture my experience will be no different from if I had actually done it, whereas in a guilt culture I will at least have my own sense of personal innocence to support me. Equally, if I have successfully concealed my wrongdoing, in a shame culture I will be unshamed, whereas in a guilt culture I should still be conscious of, and judged by, my own guilt.

Anthropologists these days tend not to see these as opposites: every culture, they believe, has shaming mechanisms and concepts of guilt, although the balance might be somewhat different in different cultures. This seems plausible: I cannot imagine a context where I could be indifferent to the false accusations of my community because I was unshakeably aware of my own innocence, or indeed of a context where an awareness of my own innocence would not make the false accusations less wounding.

If we assume, then, that what is meant is that the modern West has moved from being a strongly guilt-based culture to a strongly shame-based culture, does this explain the loss of interest in penal substitution?

I have to say that I cannot see how it does. Or, rather, I can, but only because of another cultural change that has happened around the same time: the ending of 'Christendom'. In a shame culture, what will matter to me is not that my crimes have been dealt with, so much as that they have been seen to be dealt with by my peers. So if we now live in a shame culture, the opinion of others will be what matters to me. When many in the culture around accepted that the crimes of all who believe in Christ have been dealt with (through penal substitution, or any other mechanism), then public testimony to my believing in Christ will put away shame and guilt indifferently. If the culture no longer believes the gospel, however, I will still be shamed, even if forgiven.

It seems to me that the insight that lies behind all the talk of guilt and shame cultures is far more the loss of a sense of sin in the modern West. (Alan Mann's book on the subject, *Atonement for a 'Sinless' Society*, captures the point well.) Guilt and shame alike are seen as psychological aberrations to be dealt with by counselling. For the liberal cultural elites, the same is true of most criminal behaviours (in the UK, read *The Guardian . . .*); for the more conservative popular cultures, some criminal behaviours invoke both guilt and shame, but they are few and clearly delineated (in the UK, the *Daily Mail*). The majority of people feel neither guilt nor shame in the classical anthropological senses, because they have not done anything wrong in the eyes of the culture.

This is a cultural problem for penal substitution. Telling a story that starts with criminals in the dock can work only for people who believe themselves to be criminals and are guilty and ashamed as a result.

I recall a friend when we were training for ministry (who, it should be said, was then already a far more effective evangelist than I will ever be) explaining that the gospel was that 'we had all fallen of a cliff so high that there was no chance any of us would survive . . .', at which point I stopped him and asked if this really counted as 'good news'. If the only gospel we've got solves a problem that nobody feels, then it is no wonder our churches are shrinking. There is a lot of work in first explaining to people that they really ought to be feeling guilty, before then solving the problem for them.

I should say, though, that there is a time and a place for this too. This book will come out during the 2007 commemorations of the 1807 Abolition of Slavery Act. In those evil days of European colonial oppression there were many who thought they could act with impunity in the colonies and then cover the traces of their crimes with further wrongdoing. It seems to me that a story of salvation that said to slave owners and colonial magnates that they would be exposed and dealt with, however well they had hidden their crimes, a story that confronted those who were culturally dominant, with the truth that God knew their misdeeds, was a story worth telling. And today, the child abuser who has used shame mechanisms to successfully silence his victims, and the politician who has abused her office and covered her tracks, need to be told that their guilt will not remain hidden forever, and is not insignificant, but that the cries of the victims reach the throne of God and will be heard and answered. And then they should also be told that the God who sits on the throne has a heart of love for them too, and can rescue them from their sin and guilt.

The other comment to make, again perhaps related to the colonial heritage of the West, is that in my experience, a consciousness of guilt is making a comeback, not least in the churches. Some of us have been sensitised by campaigns for trade justice and debt relief, and have become aware of the structural injustices in the world, and of the fact that we benefit from most of them. People who have been thus sensitised tend, in my experience, to derive a lot of motivation for their activities from an inescapable sense of guilt.

I was once at a ministers' conference for several days, and I found the morning and evening prayers profoundly depressing. As

I began to wonder why, I realised that the troubles of the global south had been much in our prayers, and so the resounding message, service after service, was that we were guilty. We benefited from the injustices, but we could not stop benefiting, so all that we could do in the prayers was repent again and again. There was a bunch of ministers who needed to learn to believe in penal substitution! Not so that they could ignore the injustice of the world, but so that they could know God's free forgiveness of every sin, and the joy of salvation, as they continued their struggle against the injustice of the world.

So, I think that in a society that has lost its sense of sin, penal substitution is more difficult and we need other stories of salvation also, although the penal substitution story is not rendered irrelevant. But I do not believe that our society has yet lost its sense of sin completely. Our churches certainly haven't. We need to hold on to this way of speaking of the cross also because it speaks powerfully to needs that are still real, if less universal than they once were.

As it happens, I think that the big change that ended the dominance of penal substitution around 1800 was a change away from a form of shame culture.

At that time there was an enormous shift in understandings of criminal justice, focused on the rise of the prison. In 1750, across Europe and North America, the punishment of criminals was violent and public. Hangings, floggings, and the shame of the pillory or the stocks were normal. People seemed to believe that it was important that these were all carried out in public. (In England, public hanging was abolished in 1868, public flogging in 1817 for women and 1862 for men, and the pillory in 1837.) Philosophers and theorists had been gradually criticising such punishments, and proposing their replacement with the prison as a private house of reformation, since the publication of Beccaria's celebrated *On Crimes and Punishments* in 1764. I suppose that a community that believed in the importance of public judicial violence if justice was to be done properly would find it easier to tell a story of the cross in penal terms than a community that believes in private incarceration.

If this is right, then it does not make penal substitution culturally impossible to believe, just a bit harder to believe than it was

250 years ago. It might be the case that it remains easier to believe in those few Western nations that still employ the death penalty (notably the USA), and amongst those segments of the population who believe that their own country should. This, however, is speculation.

Sin, guilt and shame

It is clear that penal substitution is no longer as resonant with our culture as it once was.

It would, of course, be possible to decry this as another instance of the paganising of culture, or to laud it as evidence of increasing civilisation; I do not think either contention is true. Or rather, I think that both are partly true. It seems to me that a culture that has forgotten what sin is, has, at the very least, become morally decadent; this damages the culture greatly and is to be mourned. On the other hand, I tend to approve of the loss of public floggings and hangings, and if that means I am going to have to be a little more inventive in preaching the cross, then that is a small price to pay.

Cultures change, and our stories of salvation must change with them. The task of theologians and preachers is to find ways of making the unchanging gospel of Jesus Christ relevant to each new generation. For a while, penal substitution was extraordinarily successful in this; now, it is still useful, but other pictures are needed as well.

This does not mean the gospel has changed (any more than the emergence of penal substitution theology during the Reformation meant the gospel had changed), just that our ways of expressing the gospel vary in their effectiveness depending on the cultural situation of our hearers. St Paul used a dozen or more different pictures to communicate to his churches; our task in speaking of the cross is, as his was (also in other contexts), to 'become all things to all people so that by all means we may save some'.

Nine – Conclusion

'Till all I do Speaks of You'

Living Under the Cross

And as hell unleashed its fury
You were lifted on a tree,
Crying 'Father God, forgive them,
Place their punishment on Me.'
Love incarnate, love divine,
Captivate this heart of mine
Till all I do speaks of you.

(Stuart Townend, 'With a Prayer'
© 2002 Thankyou Music)

The Effectiveness of the Cross

In this chapter I want to ask, very simply, what difference believing in penal substitution makes. If this is a helpful and useful story of salvation, then how will our lives, and the lives of our churches, be different because of it?

It is sometimes claimed that penal substitution makes no difference at all. The reason for this is not hard to see: if, as I have claimed, we are virtually bystanders in the story told by penal substitution, if the end of this story has us declared innocent, freed from the dock, but not changed in any other way, then it might seem that the story makes no difference to how we live. But if God is the measure of all things, then *any* theology, any account of who God is, tells us something about the *nature of things*, and so about how we should live in the world.

More: if Jesus is the definition of true humanity, as well as truly God, then any account of what Jesus did must tell us something about what it is *to be human*.

So, if penal substitution is a good story of salvation, a particular way of talking about the cross that offers us insights into who God is and how, in Jesus, he saves us, then what *does* it teach us about living in the world?

Love

The first and most important message that penal substitution (and indeed any story of salvation worth telling) will teach us is that God loves us freely, not because of anything we have done. Precisely because we are just bystanders in this story, it speaks powerfully to us of the God who demands nothing, but does everything, for our salvation. I have made this point before, but I want to emphasise it again, because the passion on both sides of recent evangelical debates about penal substitution seems to be coming from a (profoundly right) concern for this point. On the one side, critics are suggesting that penal substitution obscures the love of God and paints him instead as primarily angry, and so it is completely inadequate; on the other side, supporters are saying that penal substitution is the only way of holding on to the great gospel truth that God in Christ has done all that is necessary for our salvation.

Both claims are wrong.

I have tried to show that even when it began, with Calvin, penal substitution stressed the prior love of God as the primary reality, the reason there is a story of salvation to be told at all. I also think that other stories – Anselm's metaphor of satisfaction, the biblical picture of sacrifice, and even the strange old Greek idea of physicalism – preserve the great gospel truth that Jesus has done all that is necessary for our salvation just as well as penal substitution does. Historically, it happened that the Reformation emphasis on the completely free salvation that springs from God's love tended to be expressed in penal substitutionary terms, and this was appropriate, but not, I think, necessary. Other pictures, in different cultures, can preserve the same truth just as well.

This truth must, however, be preserved – the truth that, because of God's love known in Jesus Christ, because in Jesus

God has himself borne all the cost of our forgiveness, the gospel *is free* – God has done everything needed for our salvation in Jesus.

We can never lose sight of this. Broken and hurting people are not asked to do anything but to come, acknowledging their need, and believing, hoping against hope perhaps, that in Jesus, because of what he has done, God will accept them too. This is the promise of the gospel that can never be lost. Acceptance and salvation come freely, because God has done everything necessary already. Penal substitution is not the only story that will teach us this great truth, but it will teach it to us, and we need to keep relearning it.

Forgiveness

What penal substitution perhaps does teach us more clearly than most or all of the other stories is that forgiveness has a cost; that love hurts; that real love is not something soft and fluffy but something hard, as hard as nails.

Last Easter the BBC televised an event called *The Manchester Passion*, an excellent attempt to retell the passion of Jesus in the streets of the city using music that had come out of the recent Manchester scene. It began at the Last Supper, with Jesus amongst the disciples singing a Joy Division song, 'Love will tear us apart'.

. . . And it will. Penal substitution takes seriously this truth: God's love cost God – dearly. To forgive was not cheap and quick, but hard and painful. And so it will be for us.

When in Hosea 11 God breaks in to the courtroom scene and asks, 'How can I give you up?' this is not some saccharine moment of everyone living happily ever after, like in a Mills and Boon novel. It is much more like the painful decision of the mother of a drug addict, who, although knowing all the times her trust has been abused, remembering deceptions and thefts and casual brutalities, opens the door once more in the hope that this time it might be different. 'How many times must I forgive my brother?' asked Peter, and got the reply, 'Not seven, but seventy times seven.' And anyone who knows anything about real forgiveness will respond, 'But I couldn't bear it – that would kill me.'

And the God whom we meet in Jesus Christ knows that – better than any of us.

God calls us to forgive freely, to bear the cost and pain that forgiveness brings. And he does so only because he has done it first. The servant who has a vast debt forgiven by the king cannot keep close accounts with his fellow servants (Mt. 18:23–35); and precisely because God has borne the cost of forgiving us, he can ask us to bear the pain of forgiving one another.

Justice

Penal substitution will, of course, teach us something about justice and guilt. It will teach us first that justice cannot and will not ever be set aside. Not that there can never be forgiveness – of course not – the point of the story is precisely that there can be, and is: while crimes cannot be forgotten, yet at the same time they must also be forgiven. Cases of child abuse, where the abuser has used shaming mechanisms so successfully that none of his victims ever speak; cases of corruption, where the politician has cynically sold favours and hidden her misdeeds well enough never to be discovered; cases of war crimes, where the military officer has callously committed certain deeds, feeling secure in the knowledge that they will not come to light: these are the types of cases and situations where penal substitution becomes an important story to tell.

For the *victims* in such situations, the story of penal substitution holds the promise that there is justice in this world, even for the worst crimes, or the best-hidden atrocities. In Revelation 6 the martyrs cry out to God, 'How long, O Lord, before you avenge us?' and the response that comes is, 'Wait a little longer.'

For the *perpetrators* in these situations, the story of penal substitution holds out the invitation to stop trying to escape their crimes by their own efforts, and to find, if they dare to face up with honesty and repentance to what they have done, full and free forgiveness in Christ.

If there is a political dimension to penal substitution, it is in the recognition that justice cannot be forgotten or evaded. As those who believed in penal substitution once led the demands that the injustices of the Atlantic slave trade be ended, so now anyone who truly understands the idea will be committed to the ending of injustices in the nation and across the world.

Here are some recent examples of what I'm talking about. When I lived in London, I didn't know any evangelical church that was not involved in constant battles with the immigration authorities over the injustices of the asylum system in Britain. The recent trade justice campaign became a mass movement as part of the 'Make Poverty History' campaign, but it began small, at a rally of six thousand or so in Brighton outside the Labour Party conference one year, and I found it striking how many of those at that small rally were evangelicals.

Justice matters. It cannot be forgotten. That is one, at least, of the political implications of penal substitution.

Penal substitution will teach us, then, that no crime is irrelevant; but it will also teach us that no crime is unforgivable.

Beyond the evangelical world, Christian accounts of salvation these days often speak of promises of liberation to the oppressed, but have nothing to say to the oppressors: God is on the side of the victims, we are told, and so the victimisers find God simply against them. There is some truth in these accounts;, there is a way of talking about a 'bias to the poor' in the heart of God that is right. God does graciously bestow his presence and his help particularly on those who cannot help themselves, without question. But that cannot be the only truth. The gospel is good news for *all* people, and that means for the oppressors too. Somehow, our stories of salvation must offer the possibility of peace for abusers, oppressors and dictators as well, not only for the abused, the oppressed, and the downtrodden. And this offer, too, must be free – this peace, this salvation, will have consequences, but it comes with no conditions.

In first-century Palestine, the Romans were the occupying army, of course, but they were aided by traitors. Tax collectors who got very rich by serving as a buffer between the Romans and the people. Oppressors? Abusers? Without question. And Jesus welcomed people like that too – Matthew, and Zacchaeus. And after being welcomed by Jesus, Zacchaeus set about doing justice (Lk. 19:8).

And it must be that way around. The gospel promise is not, 'Put your life in order, and there may be hope of salvation'; it is, 'Here is hope, here is salvation, freely given to you also – now, because you have been given it, put your life in order.'

In the story of salvation that is penal substitution, we find a promise to the oppressed that justice will be done, and a promise to the oppressors that all their actions have not put them beyond the reach of God's love.

*   *   *

In Jesus God has saved us; that is what matters. We are called to live under the cross, to live lives of gratitude and worship for the wonderful thing God has done; to live lives of service and mission so that others may know the love of God also. To do those things well, we need to help one another to understand God's salvation, not completely (that is impossible) but better. I have argued in this book that Scripture and Christian history teach us that the way to do this is constantly to tell 'stories of salvation', to paint pictures of what God has done that illuminate one or another facet of that great work.

'Penal substitution' has been one such story of salvation. I have tried to argue that it is a good story, that it spoke astonishingly well to the dominant cultures or Western Europe and North America for a couple of centuries and is still relevant today, although culturally less comprehensible in the West than it once was. Unless Jesus returns first, I imagine that the time will come when it must be relegated to the history books, as a story that makes little sense to new cultures that are born. I have written this book because that time is not quite yet, and because this story gives us insights that no other story we currently have to tell does. Telling it well, we get a further glimpse of the love of God revealed in the atoning death of his Son Jesus Christ. If I have told it well enough to give some readers such a glimpse, then it has been worth the effort.

Appendix

Criticisms of and Debates about Penal Substitution

I have deliberately tried to stay away from recent evangelical debates in the course of this book, not (I hope) ignoring the issues, but (I hope) not making the issues about the personalities and the contexts. I want to end, however, with a review of one recent (American) book, and a British debate, that have both been in my mind as part of the context of writing this book.

Recovering the Scandal of the Cross?

Joel B. Green, one of the foremost evangelical New Testament scholars in the world today, and Mark D. Baker, a younger theologian, published a book together in 2000 under the title *Recovering the Scandal of the Cross: Atonement in New Testament and Contemporary Contexts*. In 2003, a British edition came out from Paternoster Press. Green and Baker argue that Christians today, if they have any understanding of atonement at all, understand it in penal substitutionary terms. They then argue that the New Testament presentation has at least five groups of images to describe the meaning of the cross, and explore four historical models (Christus Victor, Satisfaction, Moral Influence, and Penal Substitution), and two contemporary presentations (a Japanese missionary context, and an attempt to reclaim the cross within feminist theology), before asking how the atonement should be communicated today.

Green and Baker claim that we need more than one 'metaphor' of atonement to communicate the meaning of the cross successfully, and that our metaphors must be constantly changed to keep in touch with the culture we are attempting to speak to. They base their claims on the biblical text. The New Testament, they say, is a missionary text which describes the cross in a variety of ways as the needs of the mission dictate; and that should be the model of our atonement theology also.

So far, while I might have some questions of detail (particularly about the role of the history of atonement theology, and the conditions for deciding whether a metaphor is good or not), I am happy enough with Green and Baker's thesis.

Alongside this argument of theirs, however, there is another claim running: that Christians today have one monolithic view of atonement, which is penal substitution, and that this view is biblically and morally deficient and should be discarded.

Are these claims accurate?

To make any sense of the first at all (i.e. that Christians today think only in penal substitutionary terms), I guess we need to interpret Green and Baker's claims about 'Christians' as claims about *American evangelical* Christians. (I suspect, actually, that it should be even narrower than this, as many of their claims would not apply, as far as I can see, to African-American church traditions for example.) Even so, I find their argument difficult to accept. I say this with great hesitation, as I have never been to a church service in the United States, and so cannot pretend to any first-hand knowledge of the situation they are analysing. Nevertheless, the evidence they present for the claim that penal substitution has become the universal way of understanding seems to be very weak.

For example, they quote three worship songs: Philip Bliss's 'I will sing of my Redeemer', Fanny Crosby's 'To God be the Glory', and Robert Lowry's 'Nothing but the blood' as part of their evidence. Yet none of these teaches penal substitution alone.

Bliss's hymn has four verses, each expressing in simple language a different understanding of atonement: freeing from a curse; ransom; victory; and adoption. The chorus perhaps has language of 'pardon', it is true, but also speaks of 'debt' and 'purchase'. If the claim is that American evangelicals have lost sight of the many and varied metaphors of the cross in the Scriptures and focused in on penal substitution, this hymn is singularly poor evidence of that.

Fanny Crosby's 'To God be the Glory' is less focused on the atonement, but the second verse does speak of it, and does so in two ways. The first two lines contain standard redemption language: the cross of Christ purchases our freedom; the last two speak of Jesus, as judge, pardoning the offender. While this is law court language, it is some distance from classical penal substitution, because Jesus here is judge, not substitute.

Lowry's 'Nothing but the Blood' works largely with a metaphor of cleansing or washing. Other ideas are there, but penal substitution is not.

So Green and Baker might be right that American evangelicals are fixated on this idea, but the evidence they offer actually points in precisely the other direction, suggesting that in worship a rich and varied mix of biblical metaphors are regularly invoked.

This all suggests that the book might be aimed at a problem that doesn't really exist.

The more interesting and serious claims, however (at least for anyone who is not an American evangelical), are the ones about the moral character of penal substitution. But the book becomes difficult to interpret at this point, for two reasons.

First, the writers wobble somewhat between the claim that certain presentations of penal substitution are inadequate (which is certainly true, but simply uninteresting) and the claim that the idea itself is inadequate (which is certainly interesting, but simply untrue).

Second, there are two claims made about the moral deficiency of penal substitution which seem to contradict each other. At times we are told it is inadequate because it can never make any difference to the way we behave; at other times it does make a difference, and leads us to behave in appalling ways.

The first problem might be a feature of the rhetorical structure of the book. It is observable that criticisms that are first directed at a 'misunderstanding and even bizarre caricature' of penal substitution (p. 30) lead to a claim that the theory 'at the very least invites more careful articulation' (p. 32), and finally to the need to 'reject penal substitutionary atonement' (p. 93). I suppose (in part from knowing some of their other writings) that both authors do indeed want to reject penal substitution, and that the softer phrasing earlier on in the book is a way of leading readers gently to an acknowledgement of the need to do this – but I may be wrong. It may be that the target was always meant to be carica-tures only, in which case I have little problem with it.

The second problem is harder to find a way out of. On the one hand, we read a series of rhetorical questions like, 'What basis for moral behaviour remains?' and 'What significance has the cross of Christ for faith and life?' (both p. 31). We are clearly meant to answer 'None' in both cases, and so to conclude that penal sub-stitution, because it leaves us as 'bystanders' in the story, has no ethical implications at all. On the other hand, later on we find Green and Baker agreeing with the feminist criticism that penal substitution 'legitimates and perpetuates abuse in human rela-tionships' (p. 92). Well, perhaps – but if it does, it clearly does have some significance for faith and life, even if it is an unhappy significance.

The problem with this slipperiness is that it is very difficult to pin down Green and Baker's arguments. They never offer a care-ful statement of the doctrine they are criticising and then engage with it on its own terms (granted, there is a section on Charles Hodge, which the authors admit is 'a few paragraphs', and which is preceded and followed by far less careful statements). I fear that they end up criticising a gross caricature of penal substitu-tion and then dismissing any more careful presentation on that basis. I want to applaud much of what they say about the biblical basis and evangelistic use of atonement theology, but I worry that, at the heart of the book, they are being simply unfair.

The Lost Message of Jesus?

I recall exactly when I first read Steve Chalke and Alan Mann's *The Lost Message of Jesus* (Zondervan, 2003). I had been speaking at a con-ference for ministers, and one of the other speakers, a friend, said with some relish that Chalke had criticised penal substitution in his latest book and that an argument was brewing. I bought a copy of the book and read it quickly on the train home. At the end I was puz-zled – I couldn't even begin to imagine what all the fuss was about. I liked the book (I still do); I agreed with most of it (I still do); and, as far as I could see, it didn't even mention penal substitution.

Fuss there was, though.

Chalke's position as the most prominent leader within British evangelicalism meant that the book was denounced loudly in various places. The Evangelical Alliance sponsored two discussions: an evening debate, and a three-day conference at the London School of Theology (where I was asked to give a paper), and made two (I think) public statements in response to calls that Chalke be expelled. Chalke wrote an article explaining his views in *Christianity* magazine (September 2004), which did at least discuss penal substitution. Two issues later Greg Haslam, pastor of Westminster Chapel, wrote a response, and so the debate rumbled on.

Alan Mann's own book, *Atonement for a 'Sinless' Society*, appeared in 2005.

The Lost Message of Jesus is punchy and provocative. It argues that at the heart of Jesus' teaching was a concern for those forgotten by society: the poor, the weak, the marginalised, the 'sinners'. The gospel message is that God does not forget, marginalise, or judge such people, but loves and welcomes all with open arms. The kingdom of God exists when this is lived out, and the role of the church is to live this out. Chalke and Mann argue that the church has forgotten or ignored this message and this role, hence their title.

I confess that I get a bit tired of people telling churches how badly they are doing. Most of the churches I know are trying hard to do all the right things. Some could do with a bit more strategic thinking, and others need to concentrate less on keeping the wheels turning and more on what the wheels are turning for, but generally, churches are doing good. Across Britain, if homeless people are being helped, or refugees are being supported, or 'problem' teenagers are being given a place to come where they can be respected and valued, or lonely pensioners are being befriended, and so on, nine times out of ten there's a church, or at least several individual Christians, behind it somewhere. And if despairing people are finding hope in the gospel, or guilty people forgiveness in Jesus, or broken people healing from God, then ten times out of ten there's a church or Christians behind it somewhere. I don't see that the situation is very different in other countries. So I wish that Chalke and Mann had been less down on the church; I wish they'd acknowledged that the message is far from 'lost', and told some of the many stories of faithful churches doing worthwhile things. Other than that, though, it's a great book.

The book was criticised for various things.

Some people, who presumably hadn't read Genesis 1–2, objected to the idea of an 'original righteousness' that preceded 'original sin'.

Others suggested that the authors' view of repentance was wrong. The book says, 'This is what it means to repent – to begin to live another way' (p. 121) – not a complete theological definition, of course, but certainly not bad, particularly in the context of a book calling people to live out their Christian faith. Biblical repentance is not just about confession of sin, but about a change of mind and heart and life. It seems to me that the second cannot happen without the first (a change of life happens only because something has been wrong with my way of living), so calling people to the second is a fairly adequate account of what it is to 'repent'.

Other reviewers again picked up on slips of fact in the book. These are there, but (to take one example) this is hardly the first misrepresentation of St Augustine on the goodness of creation (p. 67), and the other slips are similarly anodyne, as far as I can see.

What really excited people, though, was a single sentence on page 182: 'The fact is that the cross isn't a form of cosmic child abuse – a vengeful Father, punishing his Son for an offence he hasn't even committed.' Well, of course – who ever thought otherwise? If some people found their own accounts of penal substitution being criticised in that sentence, then, frankly, they ought to change their accounts of penal substitution. But I've said enough about that already in this book.

British Debates over Penal Substitution

In the discussions that followed the publication of *The Lost Message of Jesus*, two unfortunate things happened. First, the debate became a way of playing out other arguments. It seemed to me, watching and listening, that some people who thought the

Evangelical Alliance had emphasised the 'Alliance' at the expense of the 'Evangelical' in recent years found Chalke's book useful as a way to attack that organisation without seeming to. At the same time, many 'evangelical anabaptists' used the debate as a way of expressing their own views, which often had little to do with Chalke and Mann's book. Second, most of the debate that followed accepted the position I have spent most of this book criticising, that we must try to find one right way of speaking about the cross, and reject or marginalise all the others. There was also not much evidence in the debate of a desire to hear, understand, and appreciate the arguments of people perceived to be on the 'other side'.

Since this book is the fourth piece I have written defending the idea of penal substitution, I suppose I find myself on 'the other side' to Chalke and Mann. Let me try, then, to say what is good about their positions.

In his article in *Christianity*, Chalke began with two claims: the first was that any account of the cross must have social and ethical consequences; the second, that the New Testament presentation of the atonement is 'multicoloured rather than monochrome'. The second of these has been central to my argument in this book; the first has been less central, but I hope it has been obvious that this is something I believe passionately. Later, Chalke suggests that the belief that God is love must be right at the heart of all our thinking about the cross. Again, I have insisted on this repeatedly in this book and in other work on the cross. I mentioned Alan Mann's book in chapter eight as a helpful discussion of British culture today, and of how evangelism must proceed.

So, I think Chalke and Mann get the ultimate basis of atonement theology (the love of God), its shape (many metaphors rather than one), and its necessary outcome (service, mission, and 'attitude') right. I want, then, to claim that penal substitution can be one helpful metaphor in this mix, rightly understood. Alan Mann actually accepted this, and that he had been criticising caricatures of the position, during a debate at the end of the London School of Theology conference.

Steve Chalke, as far as I am aware, would not accept this position.

Why not? Well, in his *Christianity* article, he said this: 'The theological problem with penal substitution is that it presents us with a God who is first and foremost concerned with retribution . . . although his great love motivates him to send his Son, his wrath remains the driving force behind the need for the cross.'

All I can say is that I have tried to tell a story of penal substitution in this book that is not guilty of this failing, and to point out that the classic presentations in Christian history were not guilty of it either. For example, immediately before he wrote the definitive account of penal substitution, John Calvin insisted at length that the only reason we have an atonement theology is the prior love of God. I do not recall in the course of this book writing very much about God's wrath; when I have written about it in other writings I have tried to explain it as the anger of a mother seeing her child abused. Calvin again: God is angry at sin primarily, not at sinners, and only because of that can we believe in an atonement at all.

* * *

At the London School of Theology conference that was a part of this debate, I was asked to speak about the history of evangelical atonement theology. I ended my paper with some reflections on what those of us debating the cross today could learn from those who had debated it in the past. I want to include those words here (slightly edited, as I quoted a poem that is in copyright still!) as the best thing I have to say about how to argue about the cross:

> Finally, let me just say this. As Evangelicals, we care about the cross of Jesus. It is the beginning and the heart of our faith – here we find our salvation, our hope, our motivation to live for God and to serve God in God's world. As Evangelicals we also disagree about the cross – not, mostly, about what Jesus gained for us there, but about how that was accomplished. Was it penal? Was it battle and victory? Was it governmental? Was it none of these? I have tried to give you a flavour of some of the arguments that have flowed over the past two centuries; we will have our own arguments over the next two days. I do not suppose that we will agree, any more than our predecessors could agree. The arguments are not simple or easily solved; if they were we would have solved

them by now. They are not easily solved, I believe, because the realities we talk about when we talk about the cross are so basic, so fundamental to the story of God's dealings with his creation, and to the stories of our own particular human lives. Our language and thought cannot cope with realities so large, so obvious, so basic. We do not have the perspective of heaven to make final sense of them; we have a whole series of images, pictures, stories, hints and metaphors graciously given to us by God in the Bible – and we have our stumbling attempts to make sense of them. As evangelicals we care about the cross of Jesus, we care profoundly. Because we care so much, we must have the arguments about our fumbling attempts to grasp the wonderful, awesome, life-transforming thing that God has done in Jesus, but in reading the arguments of earlier ages, I have been struck by the need, forced on us by the cross itself, which has 'broken down the walls of hostility', to argue well, lovingly, Christianly, because we argue about things that are so dear to us, so central to who we are.

It is the condition of all preachers and theologians that we seek the truths of heaven, but, being poor, we have only our dreams. Some of us care passionately that the traditions of evangelical theology, which have found in penal substitution a way of describing the release, the forgiveness, the inexpressible grace of God, should not be lost. Some of us believe passionately that, particularly in a new cultural situation, there is a real danger that penal substitutionary language could be misunderstood, and so obscure the wonders of the gospel of Christ. Thus put, I count myself in both camps. And the passion is real and appropriate – on both sides it is a passion that the cross of Christ be seen and displayed in all its wonder and glory. So – let us be passionate, yes, but also, whatever we do and say over the next hours and days, friends, let us at least try to tread softly – because we tread on one another's dreams.